Praise for *Mo*

MW00592246

"A candid heart-to-heart conve[...] can female theologian and her teenage daughter on life, love, race, loss, and faith. This engaging book shows how you can begin intergenerational dialogues in your home to explore life's mysteries and deepen faith. I highly recommend it." - Kwok Pui-lan, Ph.D., Episcopal Divinity School, Cambridge, Massachusetts

"This is a touching and moving book by mother and daughter about things that matter in life. *Mother Daughter Speak* makes biblical connections, has study questions and practical guidelines on how to deal with social concerns such as sexism, racism, climate justice, and relationships. This is a book for all ages and it is good for the mind, the heart and the soul." - Rev. Jesse Jackson, Sr., Civil Rights Activist and President of Rainbow PUSH Coalition

"Grace Ji-Sun Kim and Elisabeth Sophia Lee's *Mother Daughter Speak* is a poignant dialogue of relationships, current events, and faith. In their distinct but related voices, Kim and Lee weave an intergenerational narrative about marriage, family, loss, fear, mistakes, and gratitude that move this intimate conversation outward to encompass the realities of gender, race, religious pluralism, social media, and the environment in light of a faith that speaks to both the personal and the political." - Susan M. Shaw, Ph.D., Author of *Reflective Faith: A Theological Toolbox for Women*

"As I read the delightful, heart-breaking, up-lifting stories offered by this gifted mother-daughter writing duo, I often felt like I was reading the story of my own family. Good books introduce us to an unfamiliar world. Great books not only introduce us to a different world, but allow us to be a part of that world and learn from that world. This book is a great book. Please read together with your family to see how God works in so many different ways through so many different stories." - Soong-Chan Rah, Ph.D., Milton B. Engebretson Professor of Church Growth and Evangelism at North Park Theological Seminary

"This is a lovely memoir of family, faith, tradition, and love told through the thoughtful and thought-provoking narratives of a mother and daughter coming to terms with the joys and losses in life, all the while inviting us to reflect on how their journey may guide us to think more deeply about our own." - Jasmin Zine, Ph.D, Professor of Sociology, Wilfrid Laurier University

"In this engaging disclosure, a mother and daughter write for the head and heart as they guide us through a life's journey full of intricacies seldom discussed – the family that made us, the crises that form us and the faith that sustains us. This is a must read for those of us who know that the hand the rocks the cradle truly rules our world." - Stacey M. Floyd-Thomas is Associate Professor of Ethics and Society at Vanderbilt University and author of *Deeper Shades of Purple: Womanism in Religion and Society*

"As the father of three daughters, I've often witnessed the power of my wife's relationships with our daughters. Mother-daughter relationships can be some of the most life-giving and intimate connections on earth. In *Mother Daughter Speak*, Grace Ji-Sun Kim and Elisabeth Sophia Lee offer us a profound window into the incredible power of mother-daughter relationships." - Dr Graham Hill, Provost, Morling Theological College and author of *Global Church*

"Honest conversation between a mother and a daughter is sacred space. And in our particular cultural moment it is also a spiritual practice that calls humanity to take emotional risks to cultivate trustworthy connections with one another. This book is an act both of trust and of creativity that invites us to new and renewed ways to be well together. Would that we all have the courage to share our vulnerability with such a healing intention." - The Rev. Marcia Mount Shoop, PhD, Pastor/Head of Staff, Grace Covenant Presbyterian Church, Asheville, NC and author of *Let the Bones Dance*

mother
daughter
speak

mother
daughter
speak

lessons on life

grace ji-sun kim & elisabeth sophia lee

Published by The FAR Press

An imprint of Blaise Publications

Cleveland, Ohio

www.thefarpress.com

Printed in the United States of America

Library of Congress Control Number: 2017909475

ISBN 9780998967509

Dedication

In loving memory of *halmoni*
who gave birth to our family

Contents

Foreword by Rev. Carol Howard Merritt ii

Acknowledgements iv

Introduction 1

I. Family 5

Chapter One: Weddings and Marriages 6

Chapter Two: Honoring our Elders 16

Chapter Three: Death in the Family 23

Chapter Four: Rehearsals in Life 32

Chapter Five: Being Grateful 39

II. Life Happens 45

Chapter Six: Discrimination and Racism 46

Chapter Seven: Strategies for Life 54

Chapter Eight: Overcoming Our Fears 62

Chapter Nine: Making Mistakes 68

Chapter Ten: Rooting for the Underdog! 76

III. Church and Our Christian Faith   83

Chapter Eleven: Faith in Our World   84

Chapter Twelve: Saving the Earth   92

Chapter Thirteen: Building Relationships   97

Chapter Fourteen: Future   103

Chapter Fifteen: Social Media   110

Concluding Thoughts   117

"Three Personas" by Theodore Andrew Lee   118

Foreword

My daughter, Calla, and I go for a walk each day near our home in Chattanooga, Tennessee. She insists on a mile, even when I complain that I'm exhausted from work. We plod along on an old wooden bridge that can no longer bear the burden of cars, so pedestrians stroll, enjoying the dusk. As our steps move along the boards in a soft rhythm, the details of her day spill out. I hear about her friends, teachers, and work. The social maneuverings of adolescence seem as puzzling now as they did when I was a teenager. As the words flow above the bridge, the water courses beneath our feet, glistening. The setting sun is bright and dancing along the river's ripples.

I breathe in the cool air, and I want to inhale the entire moment. I long to somehow consume it, so that it becomes a permanent part of me, because this time between mother and daughter feels too fleeting. The eighteen years that Calla is under my care is too short. There is too much to do, teach, and instill. There is never enough room in the day for the enormity of the task of parenting and loving my daughter.

I look around and this world seems to be such a complicated place from this perspective. Parents try to react to the emerging contexts of social media, environmental degradation, dynamic immigration, and economic disparities. Many of the social ills of racism, sexism, and classism persist and seem to grow stronger. As Christians, we know that these injustices will need to be tended to, from generation to generation. So we walk, moving along each subject. I try to instill some awareness and compassion; Calla teaches me, regularly pointing out my blind spots. We handle each topic, dissecting and disagreeing. I want her to be able to negotiate and look at things critically and respectfully. We work on that delicate balance of empowerment and empathy which is so important for mothers and daughters.

It's difficult. We need the wisdom of generations. We long for the voices of sisters and wise parents to model what these conversations could look like and what form they should take. We need people who can express the importance of shared suffering as well as delight in the movement of a beautiful dance. When we yearn for these things, Rev. Dr. Grace Ji-Sun Kim and Elisabeth Sophia Lee echo back.

In their book, Mother Daughter Speak, Kim and Lee show us how to have these conversations of delight and sorrow, empowerment and humility. Kim and Lee guide on our journeys, and as our footsteps plod, we can heed their voices. I read their discussions with great interest, appreciating each story and understanding more and more about the intimate and mysterious bond that mothers and daughters share.

Rev. Carol Howard Merritt

Acknowledgments

Writing a book is never easy. Co-writing brings additional challenges. We spent a great deal of time in discussion and writing. Negotiations and renegotiations and further negotiations occurred as we co-wrote this book. But as we went through the many stages of writing and rewriting, our family was always there for us. They helped and supported us from the conception of this project right through to its publication. Their aid helped sustain us as we worked on this book together.

Our family's lives are interwoven in this book. We are thankful to each family member, Perry (husband and dad) and Theodore and Joshua (sons and brothers), who allowed us to share parts of their lives. Our immediate family has not only been a source of support for our writing, but they also served as a source of content for the book. Much of our lives are reflected together in these writings. We are thankful for their openness to talk about their struggles and how we continue to build and grow a strong family.

It was a good experience to have contributions from our family. Our writing ended up strengthening our family bonds.

We are grateful for the many people who have helped us along the way. We are grateful to The FAR Press and editors Gina Messina and Xochitl Alvizo for their kindness and provision from the beginning of the book project. They cleared the road and skillfully guided us in the creation of this book of shared stories. We are happy to have worked with them on such a personal, impactful, and enlightening project.

We are thankful to family and friends: Naomi Bu,

Bruce Marold, Mark Koenig, David Hershey and Daniel Mudd, who have read all or parts of our book and have given us valuable suggestions. We are grateful to Theodore Andrew Lee and Naomi Bu who codesigned our beautiful book cover. We also thank Sojourners and Feminist Studies in Religion for permission to reprint my (Grace) previously published blog posts.

Lastly, we want to thank each other for this wonderful journey of writing and building this book together. Mother thanks daughter. Daughter thanks mother. Relationships are always works in progress. We are thankful for each other's lives as we journey together in this walk we call life.

Introduction

Mother-daughter relationships can be wonderful and powerful. They can also be stressful, challenging, and painful. They are often delicate and tender. Ours is all of those things. My daughter is now sixteen years old, but I clearly remember the day that she was born. Of my three pregnancies, she was the easiest, the least traumatic delivery. Giving birth to her was a moment of profound and lasting joy for me.

She came into the world very gracefully and as if her 'time had come.' She was born on exactly the date that my doctor had predicted. She was born beautiful and I went home from the hospital with tremendous joy and fulfillment.

Then, the difficulties began. She was born with jaundice, so I had to take her to the doctor every day to have her blood checked. He would stick a needle in her heel and she would scream. It was a trying couple of weeks until my mother finally said, 'All Korean babies have jaundice, so stop taking her to the doctor every day.' I stopped, and eventually her skin cleared up.

A breast-feeding crisis followed. She consumed a lot but shortly after she finished nursing, she would throw up all the milk. It was as if her body couldn't help regurgitating the liquid. As soon as I lifted her up to burp her, the milk would start gushing out of her mouth. I worried that no nourishment was staying in her small, fragile body.

Now, as I look back at how she has grown into a beautiful teenager despite those concerns and a thousand others since, I have a profound thankfulness in my heart for her birth, her growth into a thoughtful young woman, and her life. Our relationship has its bumps and trials, but it is filled with kindness and joy.

I am a daughter of an immigrant family. In 1975, my parents left everything they had in South Korea with hopes and dreams of making a new life in our adopted land, Canada. I was five years old when our family boarded the plane in South Korea to immigrate to Canada.

My mother was a quiet and reserved woman. She never said anything trivial or unimportant. Her quiet personality defined our relationship. Because my mother was quiet, I never knew much about how she was feeling. Her quietness had something to do with the patriarchal world in which she lived. I knew she lived in fear of my father who constantly told her to obey him. He made it clear to her that "if you do not obey, you will suffer the consequences." This made life difficult for my mother and eventually created grave tensions between us too.

But her quietness also had to do with her inability to assimilate into the white community, largely due to her lack of fluency in English. Most of the difficulty between my mother and me also resulted from this absence of a language that we shared with equal facility. My mother spoke Korean, and responding in the same language became harder and harder for me to do as I learned English at school and used it on a regular basis. The challenge of communication highlighted the difficulty I faced living between two cultures. Indeed, much of my life has straddled the Korean and Euro-American cultures.

Then in 2010 my mother was suddenly diagnosed with stage four lung cancer though she had never smoked in her life. She died painfully six months after the diagnosis when she was only sixty-four years old and I was forty. Her sudden death left me suspended above an abyss. I couldn't function properly for six months; to hide my sorrow from view, I wore sunglasses for two months and couldn't eat properly for a year.

Her death left a huge void in my life and in my heart. I had never really had a deep conversation with my mom about her broken-hearted experiences and her silent suffering added an extra layer of sadness to my grief. The suddenness of her death and the enormity of my loss suffocated my spirit. I had always imagined that later in life I'd have a stronger relationship with my mother and she'd be able to share some of her deepest wounds, pains, and struggles with me. Her death robbed me of that possibility.

But her death did inspire me to forge a stronger relationship with my own children. I try to share some of my personal hardships with them so that they will know my story and the story of our family. This is part of the reason for writing this book with my daughter.

Daughters need to communicate with their mothers and mothers with their daughters. Relationships need to develop. We have tried to do that here. Our wish for you, the reader of this book, is that you will communicate and share your feelings, ideas, and hopes with your family members while you still can.

Family

Chapter One

Weddings and Marriages

"A Dream Wedding Day"
Elisabeth Sophia Lee

"If I speak in the tongues of mortals and of angels, but do not have love, I am a noisy gong or a clanging cymbal. And if I have prophetic powers, and understand all mysteries and all knowledge, and if I have all faith, so as to remove mountains, but do not have love, I am nothing. If I give away all my possessions, and if I hand over my body so that I may boast, but do not have love, I gain nothing."

- 1 CORINTHIANS 13:1-3

Being a teenage girl, I have naturally dreamt about the day of the white dress, the vows, and the ring: my wedding day. I talk about it with my friends and wonder what it will be like. We search through pictures on the Internet and admire celebrity wedding photos.

I dream about my wedding day all the time. I think about the beautiful flower arrangements that will embellish the church and banquet hall. I picture the wedding cake. I like simple things, so I want my cake to look understated and elegant. I imagine my father walking me down the aisle toward my soon-to-be husband. We girls watch beauty pageants, see photoshopped advertisements and young girls modeling for fashion editorials, and we learn at a young age that women are largely judged by how they look and how they dress. We are told our big day will be like a fairy tale—a day on which our Prince Charming will sweep us off our feet. Of course, I imagine the countless different styles of wedding dresses that I might wear on that day. My cousin, Naomi, is engrossed in fashion, so I have imagined her designing my gown. I sometimes flip through wedding magazines when I sit in a Barnes and Noble bookstore, just to look at the beautiful dress designs. I cannot believe that I must choose only one when the time comes. I elaborate upon my dreams by thinking about the never-ending possibilities for colors and designs of my bridesmaids' dresses.

I often look through my mom's wedding album. I have to beg her to show them to me. She has these huge weddings albums hidden in her walk-in closet. I often ask her why they are stashed in her closet and she just replies that is the best place to store them. I think they shouldn't be stored but displayed! My mom looked stunning in all the pictures. She had a lovely simple dress and veil. Her bouquet was exactly how I would like my own to be. I often wonder what she was feeling on her wedding day. What was she experiencing and thinking as she walked down the aisle? Was she nervous? Excited? Was she scared? A few years ago, my mom bought a beautiful diamond Tiffany necklace to celebrate her book publication. It is my mom's favorite piece of jewelry; she never takes it off. To my delight, my mom said she would pass on that necklace to me on my wedding day. I am thrilled about the necklace and all the things that will make my wedding day memorable.

I know a lot of girls fantasize about their wedding day. My mom said when she was a little girl, she also imagined her wedding day by looking at wedding dress magazines and clipping out her favorite dresses. This was all exciting for her until she realized that the cost of the dresses that she liked were way beyond her budget.

When I talk about weddings with my mom, she tells me the wedding day itself is not that important, that I should not live in a fairy tale but ground myself in reality. My mom often tells the story of her aunt saying, "People get married because they love each other. But marriage is so tough; it takes more than loving each other. It takes a lot of work. It will not always be like a bed of flowers; it will be difficult." In other words, the wedding day is important for many people, but it is marriage that should be the focus. The wedding day is just the first day of your marriage. Marriage is more than a one-day event. It is a beginning of living out a commitment between two partners, a public commitment made in the presence of friends and family. Wedding days are a doorway to a life of giving and taking, learning to love, and learning to negotiate. As my mom goes on and on talking about marriage, my dreams of my wedding day shift and I begin reimagining.

I guess it is important to realize that what follows the wedding day is more important than the big day. Young girls like me should focus on both the wedding day and the life that follows. It is not through magazines but through talking to those –like my mom who are already married that we can begin to imagine the highs and lows of that reality and prepare for it.

"Marriage: For Whom is it, Really?"
Grace Ji-Sun Kim

"Therefore a man leaves his father and his mother and clings to his wife, and they become one flesh."

- GENESIS 2:24

"You don't marry to make yourself happy, you marry to make someone else happy... Marriage isn't for you. It's not about you. Marriage is about the person you married."

- SETH ADAM SMITH

     I read Seth Adam Smith's post, "Marriage isn't for you"[1] and I found myself wondering whether it really speaks to women today. A few years ago, Smith's post exploded on the Internet and went viral. Subsequently, he was invited to speak about his blog post on several television programs. The media seemed to love his post about marriage, but it never sat well with me. While his assertion diminishes the importance of the self in favor of advantaging the other, it denies one the expectation of entering into marriage anticipating being able to enjoy the rewards coming from having a partner. Smith's emphasis is a sophism, easily unmasked. I showed my daughter the blog post and asked her to think about it. I showed it to her, because she is like many young girls who have big dreams of their wedding day. She dreams about the dress, the flowers, and the dance. Young girls dream about the big day, but forget to think about what follows — marriage. So I showed my daughter the blog post to see if it is helpful to women or not? She did not respond right away, but she did admit the post sounded

1 Seth Adam Smith, "Marriage isn't for you." Retrieved from: http://sethadamsmith.com/about/.

'romantic.' Her comment affirmed that young girls are romanticizing marriage and are not in touch with the reality and necessity of partnership and equality in a marriage. Instead, they think of marriage in fairy tale terms: the woman gets her prince and lives happily ever after. Indeed, that is nothing but a fairy tale.

While I imagine that Seth most likely is a great husband, and his wife of one-and-a-half years (at the time of his post) is probably content, I question whether he has sufficiently deep insight at this point in their marriage to address the real-life crises and realities of marriage. He has been married less than two years. What wisdom does he have to give to those who have gone through the tribulations of childbirth, child loss, job loss, death, separation, or divorce? Unfortunately, not much. Let's go even deeper into Smith's proposition.

Smith quotes his father on what marriage is about:

My dad giving his response to my concerns was such a moment [when Seth had concerns about marrying his fiancé, he had this discussion with his dad] for me. With a knowing smile he said, "Seth, you're being totally selfish. So I'm going to make this really simple: marriage isn't for you. You don't marry to make yourself happy, you marry to make someone else happy. More than that, your marriage isn't for yourself, you're marrying for a family. Not just for the in-laws and all of that nonsense, but for your future children. Who do you want to help you raise them? Who do you want to influence them? Marriage isn't for you. It's not about you. Marriage is about the person you married." [2]

This is a beautiful proposition, but I think it is oversimplified and tells only half of the story. Historically, marriage has generally been about a woman leaving her

---

2 Smith, "Marriage isn't for you."

family to become part of a man's household so that he now had ownership over her. She married to have children and to help continue the patriarchal lineage. In the Asian context, a woman left her parents' family to join the family of her husband. Her name was moved to the husband's family book. She now belonged to her husband's family as property and was treated as such. Even if she was unhappy, there was no way for her to return to her family of origin. She was obliged to remain part of her husband's family. I shared with my daughter how fortunate she is to be living in a society where this is no longer the norm. Women have rights in marriage and are no longer thought of as property to be traded or bought. I don't think she realized how lucky she is. She has only seen the new "norm," which, in general, is that women are free to make choices in a marriage.

In that unfortunate historical context, yes, "marriage isn't for you. It's not about you. Marriage is about the person you married"— except the man in the marriage was not expected to reciprocate that level of sacrifice. In his eyes, it was all about him and his family. While I am fairly certain Smith did not mean to evoke that arrangement, his statement, at face value, does suggest that one must enter marriage as an act in which one gives up part of oneself.

Women had to endure this for centuries, and even in the West much of this viewpoint is assumed in present-day marriage. Women are socialized to sacrifice themselves and their bodies to carry and deliver babies; childbirth really isn't about a woman's body, it is about the survival of the family into which you married. In addition, women are told to give up their careers or education for the sake of raising their children. I still remember my wedding day as if it happened yesterday. It was the summer I graduated from my Master of Divinity program and I was planning to begin my Ph.D. that fall. My husband was nearing the end of his Ph.D. program in Mechanical Engineering. Neither of us had jobs, but we did have student debt! We married, financed by a laughably small amount of money in the bank.

Since I didn't have much money, I bought nice wedding dress material and a woman at my church made the dress for me. My wedding cake was made by a friend who is a baker and the wedding reception was held at the church. I had so little budget for my own wedding that I always thought, if I ever have a daughter, I hope I can have enough funds to give her a 'proper' wedding, by which I meant that I hoped she'd be able to go out and buy the cake and dress and reception she wants instead of relying on the goodness of her friends. Even though I didn't have an expensive wedding, I still spent significant time planning. The task was enormous as neither my parents nor my in-laws did much to help me. I carried the weight of the wedding planning on my shoulders.

We had over six hundred guests. My dad invited all of his past and present friends, which included his school alumni, a big deal for Koreans (this is a common practice for many Korean immigrant families). Then we had to invite everyone from the church where I worked, and the people from the church that my parents attended. All in all, about six hundred people attended our wedding! The day was chaotic, undeniably stressful—and lovely. The day is now a delightful memory. Our premarital counseling was incredibly brief — so brief, I don't remember much about it. My minister met with us once, we did a personality test, and we met one more time afterwards as a follow up. That was it. As I think about my own daughter, I hope she will have more extensive, rigorous counseling so that she will be certain this is the path for her. The goal should be to prevent surprises in the marriage which could have been addressed in the counseling sessions.

Looking back, I think we should have spent more time on premarital counseling and less on wedding planning. That is what I want to pass on to my three children, but especially to my daughter. The wedding day itself is not such a big deal. It is just one day. The hope is that the marriage will be for a lifetime. As such, the majority planning and thinking should focus on after the wedding day, when real life and difficulties hit. Life is not just a wedding day full of picture taking, eating, smiling, greeting, dancing, and hugging. Life is about the journey, the hardships and joys. I experienced some struggles right after our wedding day, when my hands broke out in terrible eczema. The skin was ripping, bleeding, and becoming infected. I had to wear gloves to prevent myself from scratching all day and night. I was miserable.

This infirmity in my hands shaped what I could and could not do around the house. My in-laws were not happy about this as they expected me to fulfill the 'wifely' or domestic duties around the house. My mother kept apologizing to them, saying I had never had eczema until I got married. This was true. This awful eczema lasted for about eight years after my marriage. My husband tried his best to shield me from his own family. That was only the beginning of the problems I faced in my marriage. Cultural and social expectations were woven throughout my life, making marriage harsh and difficult.

Even today as I look around I am often reminded of the difficulties married people face, especially women. As middle-aged women go through mid-life crises, they are expected to stay in loveless marriages. In one way or another, they're constantly reminded that "marriage isn't about you," it's about your children, your spouse's career, and your family's role in society.

The church does this too. It often tells women living in abusive relationships to stay in their marriages, because "marriage isn't about you. It is about the family." The implication is that it'd be better for the women to stay in a risky relationship than to break up the family. This has always been a fear of mine: that my own daughter may become trapped in an abusive relationship. Because she's still a young teen, I haven't discussed this too deeply yet with her, but as she gets older, it is something I want to do. Timing is important; to discuss such sensitive issues our daughters need to be ready. Yet even high schoolers can find themselves in an abusive situation.

Seth Smith's aphorism, that marriage isn't about you, it's about your spouse or the children, has been drilled into women. In some ways, what he says is true. In marriage, we do make sacrifices and compromises for each other. So I think Seth got it half right.

The half Seth missed is that marriage is also about "me." Marriage is about the happiness of individuals: their careers, their bodies, and their own fulfillment and love. If marriage were all about selflessness, it would be better to join a convent that trains nurses to take care of the poor. My daughter has her own dreams of getting married one day, and joining a convent is not part of her dream. If we cannot think about our own inner beings, what does that lead us to believe about marriage? Marriage becomes nothing but a patriarchal reenactment of ancient times. Instead, in order to fulfill one's partner, one must have a fulfilled life oneself.

Healthy marriages will always involve sacrifices for one's partner, but we also have to look out for our own happiness. Leaving "me" out of marriage is a dangerous thing — for me, for my spouse, and for our shared life. We must move away from the notion that "only the other is important." Instead, the relationship must be mutual, reciprocal. Marriage is about both partners. It is not about you—and it is not about me; and it is also totally about you—and it is totally about me.

Reflections:

1. What are some of the difficulties and challenges in your own marriage or partnership? How can you overcome such challenges? How do you sustain your relationship so that both people feel content, happy, and loved?

2. How do we make marriage equal, so both partners feel that they are equal partners in love?

3. What does true partnership look like?

4. If you are a parent, how does parenting affect your marriage?

5. If you are a young person, do you dream about the details of your wedding day? What does your "big day" look like?

6. How have movies and television influenced your view of marriage? Should we rethink marriage in light of the movies and television?

7. What have you learned from your parent(s) about marriage? Where else can we find good role models to help us think about marriage?

8. How are Christians supposed to understand love and marriage? What does 1 Corinthians 13:1-3 mean in the context of marriage?

Chapter Two

Honoring Our Elders

"Halmoni"
Elisabeth Sophia Lee

*"Honor your father and your mother, so that your days may be
long in the land that the Lord your God is giving you."*

- EXODUS 20:12

I did not know my grandmother's actual name and
I never thought to ask her. We called her *halmoni*, which
means grandmother in Korean. As I grew up, I learned her
Korean name. But I rarely spoke her Korean name and she
didn't have an English one. In the Korean tradition, it is
very rude to refer to adults by their first name. One would
never talk about an adult by their first name, let alone
address them by it. In most cases, one doesn't even know
one's grandparents', uncles', aunts', and older cousins' given
name, as it is inappropriate to use it. One just addresses
them by their role or status— aunt, uncle, older cousin, etc.

My grandmother was a very lovely and kind woman.
She was smart, gentle, and caring to my brothers and me.
My mother used to tell me that I looked like my grandmother. She said that I had the same eyes and face shape.
My grandmother was tall and had short, black, curly hair.
My grandmother lived in Toronto, Canada with my aunt
and her family, but sometimes she came down to Pennsylvania to visit us. Whenever she came, she always took care
of my family and me. While we were at school or work, she
prepared countless yummy Korean meals and cleaned our

house until it was spotless. To this day, I can still imagine the sweet, mouth-watering aromas that wafted through all three levels of our house when she was in town.

My grandmother's first language was Korean and she could barely speak English. When she spoke the little English she knew, she did so with a strong Korean accent, which made it difficult for my brothers and me to communicate with her. The language barrier never stopped us from loving and caring for each other, though. Love is understood everywhere by everyone. My parents were often at work and busy with things, so my grandmother was like a second parent to me. She filled the role of "mother" when she came to visit. My mother always appreciated this, as she was extremely busy with teaching and doing her own work. Looking back, I realize how much my halmoni did for us and wish I could've done more for her before she passed away.

My *halmoni* was very funny. One time, I was drinking milk, and something she said made me laugh and laugh—so much so, that the milk came out of my nose. This only made us laugh more! Anyone else would have chastised me for spilling milk on our couch. But this wasn't anyone else. It was my *halmoni*.

My *halmoni* let my younger brother and me play all the time. If we accidentally broke something small, she wouldn't yell or get mad. She was always full of forgiveness. That said, my mom always thought that my *halmoni* spoiled us. She thought my halmoni should be stricter instead of letting us get away with everything. I have to say, I really liked the fact that my grandmother spoiled us. My parents were rather strict with us, so it was nice to have someone who wasn't.

She was the kindest grandmother I ever knew.

When my parents disciplined me or my brothers, my grandmother felt so heartbroken, she would intervene and whisk us away into another room. She would hug us while we wailed. She would comfort us and tell us that everything would be alright. She was such a wonderful grandmother to me.

My grandmother taught me many important life lessons, among them, to laugh more and to care for each other more. I knew that she always cared about my mother and my family. Otherwise, she would not have spent so much time with us when my mother was busy with her new teaching position.

My grandmother cared for others and tried her best to be kind to everyone around her. Even if someone did not treat her well, she didn't respond harshly but rather showed kindness. My mother would often share with my *halmoni* her pain and anger at Korean American moms saying hurtful things to her about her parenting skills and being a 'working mom'. My mother was often upset by such negative comments, and so she complained to my grandmother about them. But my grandmother never had ill feelings toward the other women. She told my mother to calm down and ignore what they were saying. She'd say, "There's no need to be hostile or angry towards them." I know my mother had a hard time accepting my grandmother's advice but she followed it anyway. My grandmother kept saying that we should show kindness to those who hurt us.

My *halmoni* left us a legacy of kindness and gentleness. I will always remember her for her goodness, which spread to everyone around her. As I think about the biblical passage of honoring our parents, I know that we must do all that we can to do that. A part of that includes honoring our elders and those who came before us.

"Mother's Day"
Grace Ji-Sun Kim

"Honor your father and mother"— this is the first command-ment with a promise"

- Ephesians 6:2

I can only imagine how terrifying and difficult it was for my mom to bring her two little girls on a plane from Korea to Alaska, then Hawaii, and then the Toronto Pearson Airport… only to find my dad wasn't there to pick us up. As usual, he was late. It was January 17, 1975 when we emigrated from Korea to Canada. My dad had arrived in Canada a month earlier.

I still remember the day we left Korea. My paternal grandmother (*chin-halmoni*) said the flight would be very long and there would be no restrooms on the plane. She made me sit in the bathroom for a very long time in hopes I would not have to go again until I landed in Canada. I remember my uncle (*keun-ah-buh-gi*) giving my sister and me very pretty necklaces (which I still have) inscribed with personal information, just in case we got lost. I remember being in the airport with uncles, aunts, and cousins who came out to say their goodbyes. All of our family members were weeping – especially my grandmother. They thought they would never see us again.

Since I was only five, I didn't realize the impact that day would have on the rest of my life. My mother was only twenty-nine and she did not know what was waiting for her as she left Korea. She left her entire family to join my dad — against the wishes of all his family, for it was his idea to leave Korea and emigrate to Canada. She left behind every-thing she knew: her family, her house, her community, her friends, her culture, and her history in order to start afresh in a new and foreign land. I can only imagine the fear in her heart as she obeyed my father. In a Confucian context where obedience was crucial, it was expected that women obey men. When a girl was young, she was to obey her father; when married, she obeyed her husband; and when a widow, her son. This level of obedience was embedded in Asian culture. It was something that was fully expected of my own mother. She was to obey my father. When I tell this Confucian tradition to my daughter, she is in disbelief. As she grows up in this western culture, she cannot seem to grasp the fact that women had to be so obedient to men. As many first generation immigrants can imagine given their own experiences, it was not an easy life for our family. Canada was not the "land of milk and honey" that everyone had told us it would be. Rather, it was tough and sometimes heart-wrenching to be there.

We landed in Toronto in January during one of the harshest winters in recent memory. We were so cold and miserable; I remember wanting to stay indoors all day long. During that time, I started kindergarten and remember being mocked by others who did not know "what" I was. Many Canadians asked if I were Chinese or Japanese. When I told them I was Korean, they said, "What is Korean? You can't be Korean. You are Chinese or Japanese." They used other, less polite terms to describe me, too. Without any knowledge of English, I was a constant target of racism.

I can only imagine the frequent regret my mother must have felt as she and her children experienced the isolation, loneliness, and sense of hopelessness of trying to adjust to an unfamiliar land, a land that did not welcome her or her family. Her suffering, caused by prejudice, racism, and sexism, she endured silently. She never openly shared her pain even though it was visible on her face and her body. Like many Korean immigrant women, she suffered in silence and alone. My children are not always aware of the many difficult experiences of first generation immigrants. Therefore, I always try to do my best to remind them of the difficulties that my own mother had faced as an immigrant. She faced racism every day and it took a toll on her life. It is important that we remember our past as it affects our present and our future. I want my daughter to be grateful for the sacrifices that my own mother made to leave Korea for a more hopeful future in North America. I want my daughter to understand the sacrifices as well as the kindness that my mother showed to her grandkids, but also the pain that she had to endure as an immigrant.

Amidst of all these difficulties and obstacles, my mom did her best to raise my sister and me. She didn't complain about her situation but set about the task of providing for us, even as we became adults.

When I was raising my own family, she was a kind, compassionate, giving, and caring mother. She stayed with me a few months a year to help with the cooking, cleaning, and the raising of my three children. She taught them Bible stories and showed them love, grace and kindness. It was a sacrifice for my mother to stay with us for those months, as she enjoyed her busy, independent life in Toronto.

My mother passed away on January 12, 2010 after fighting a battle with lung cancer. Now, I can only wonder about her sorrows, as she did not share with me her own personal stories or dreams not yet realized. I am sad I will never be able to understand fully her deep struggles. I hope for something differently for my daughter and me. I make it a priority to share freely with her, to be sure she will know her own family history and story and not have to "imagine" as I must do for many things.

What I know for sure about my mom is her hard work ethic, diligence, determination, and perseverance that enabled her to survive faithfully in a foreign land. I don't have to imagine her deep love for God, her strong commitment to the church, her constant prayer, and her love for her community and family because I saw her live out those values each and every day. Her Spirit-Chi[1] lives on, as I know it does within me and my own three children.

Reflections:

1. In what ways do you have good relationships with your parents, or grandparents? How do you strengthen your relationships with your parents and grandparents while you still can?

2. What special relationships do you have with elders inside or beyond your family circle? What makes these relationships special, and how do you continue to nurture them?

3. In what ways are your relationships with your children healthy? If they are unhealthy, what might you do to strengthen and improve those relationships?

---

1 Spirit-Chi is the Spirit that exists in all of us which gives us energy, warmth and life. For more discussion on Spirit-Chi please see my book, *The Holy Spirit, Chi, and the Other* (Palgrave Macmillan, 2011).

Chapter Three

Death in the Family

"Losing *Halmoni*"
Elisabeth Sophia Lee

"Jesus said to her, "I am the resurrection and the life. Those who believe in me, even though they die, will live, and everyone who lives and believes in me will never die. Do you believe this?"

- JOHN 11:25-26

My grandmother was so loving, gentle, and kind to my brother and me that it broke my heart in the summer of 2009 to find out that my *halmoni* had lung cancer. The scary news shocked everyone in our family; we never expected it. She had always been so healthy and had never smoked in her life. How could this be?

My mother was in such shock, she kept grandmother's cancer a secret from us for four months. She simply couldn't believe her own mother, who never smoked, could have lung cancer. She also wanted to spare my brothers and me the stress of knowing that our *halmoni* was dying.

The cancer slowly spread through her left lung and soon took over both lungs. As the cancer progressed, her treatment progressed. She began by only making occasional visits to the hospital, mainly check-ups. Then she started chemotherapy and lost all her hair. A couple of months later in November, my grandmother collapsed in the kitchen while washing dishes. She was rushed to the ER, and the doctors discovered she had suffered a stroke. Things had taken a turn for the worse. The cancer was incurable, and she was losing her ability to walk and talk.

In December, my family and I went to visit her. My brothers and I were very young and scared, and we didn't know what to expect. We slept at our aunt's house, but we frequently visited our grandmother at the hospital. The most devastated person was my mother. She was horrified and terrified of what was happening to my grandmother. I tried to make sure that my mother was alright during my grandmother's illness.

The smell of the hospital is still vivid to me, like the mixture of the medicine and yogurt we fed my grandmother while she was there. We tried to spend as much time with her as possible, knowing our time was limited. Eventually, we had to return home to Pennsylvania because our Christmas break was ending. It was very difficult to say goodbye.

A few weeks later, we got a call from our aunt. She said our grandmother had stopped breathing. My aunt was begging the doctor to do something but there was nothing the doctor could do. Meanwhile, my family and I quickly packed our things, some black clothing (just in case), and drove eight-hours to Toronto, Canada. Unfortunately, we were too late. My grandmother had already passed away. My dad drove slowly to my cousins' house. It was hard to believe she was gone. Our entire family broke down in pain and grief. We were devastated.

I wondered how my mom felt about losing a huge part of her life, her mother. We were all so emotional I didn't have the courage to ask her.

For the next few days, we planned my grandmother's funeral. We invited friends and family. The next weekend we dressed in black and went to the church for the funeral. At the front of the chapel lay my grandmother, peacefully in her coffin. She was expertly made up and attired in the traditional Korean dress called *hanbok*. No one would have guessed she had been in such pain.

The funeral was the saddest event I have experienced in my young life. It was also the first funeral I attended. After the service, we went to the cemetery and buried my grandmother. It was heartbreaking; I couldn't watch. To this day, I feel empty. My grandmother was everything to me.

We visit my grandmother's grave every time we go to Canada. The visits bring back good memories which make me smile. I find comfort in knowing my grandmother is doing better now and is not suffering. I wish I could see my grandmother's face again, just one more time. Losing her made me realize life is short, and you never know when it can be taken away from you. We need to spend every moment like it's the last. We need to make every moment count for something.

"Prayer"[1]
Grace Ji-Sun Kim

"Which of you fathers, if your son asks for a fish, will give him a snake instead? Or if he asks for an egg, will give him a scorpion?"

- LUKE 11:12

Praying is difficult.

I will never forget receiving a frantic call from my sister in Canada; a call I never imagined I would receive in my lifetime. She said our mom had gone to the doctor with some health issues and they had discovered she had stage four lung cancer.

The younger the patient, the more aggressive is the cancer.

My mother was only sixty-three and had always been very healthy. She always ate a healthy diet, exercised, and never smoked. She often encouraged us to do likewise. Whenever she visited our family, she would give my three children lots of green, leafy vegetables for lunch and dinner. She was, for all intents and purposes, a "health nut!"

Despite all that, she developed lung cancer. She had a cough for several months, but she thought it was simply a bad cold. Looking back, she should have visited a doctor sooner than she did. By the time she finally visited the doctor and was diagnosed, it was too late. Our family fell into the depths of despair and sorrow.

1 This is a modified version of an essay on prayer that I wrote for *What Did Jesus Ask?: Christian Leaders Reflect on His Questions of Faith.* Foreword by Nancy Gibbs, edited by Elizabeth Dias (New York: Time), 177-180.

Of my three children, my daughter took it the hardest. She was the closest to my mother and always wanted to be with her. She never wanted to leave after visits. She was, by far, the most emotionally attached to my mother. So, when she found out that her grandmother had cancer, she was devastated.

In times of our deepest pain and despair, what is there left to do but cry out to God for relief? As Christians, our family prayed for healing. Yet my mother's health only grew worse. She had a stroke that left her mute and largely immobile. Did God even hear our prayers? Many Christians pray fervently and still watch loved ones die. And yet Christians continue to pray. Why do we continue to pray when it appears God is not answering? What will praying do?

Some of us view prayer as a free store where we grab anything we want, the God to whom we pray as a divine Santa Claus who grants our wishes. However, we soon realize our prayers are not answered exactly as we ask. During those times, we feel anxious and unsettled. Why isn't God answering my prayer? There is only silence and more silence.

Our family, friends, and church members all prayed for my mother. And God did not answer our prayers. In the midst of this self-doubt, I came upon this Lukan passage, and I made it my own.

> *"Which of you fathers, if your son asks for a fish, will give him a snake instead? Or if he asks for an egg, will give him a scorpion?"*

Jesus assures us that God is much like a parent who only gives his or her children what is good. When I tell my daughter I love her more than anything in the world, understandably she cannot grasp the depth of this love. I hope that one day she will come to understand that God's love is even greater than this.

All that said, we persist in prayer because Jesus implies that if a human parent is wise and loving enough not to give a scorpion to a beloved child who wants an egg, then surely God will not either. Why? Because God is the "ultimate good," the one who is greater in love than all human parents. As Jesus says, "If [we] then, who are evil, know how to give good gifts to our children, how much more will the heavenly Father give the Holy Spirit to those who ask him!" If simple humans can give "good gifts," won't the great and good God offer even more?

I found this scripture comforting as I experienced the pain of my mother's illness and death. This question about eggs and scorpions encourages us to hang on. It reignites our faith that God's love is greater than anything we can imagine. Instead of our own impatient way, we need to rely on God and wait upon God's timing. A way to wait upon God is through prayer.

My own children were afraid of what might happen to their grandmother. Because my daughter was the closest to my mother of my three children, I could see that she would be most affected by her sickness and eventual passing. As I prayed for my mother, I also prayed for my children. One night as we prayed as a family, my daughter prayed for healing. She prayed that grandmother would be all better again. This prayer broke my heart.

Prayer is a matter of faith. I tried to teach my girl that prayer is a way of sustaining our faith in God, more than asking for something. As a young girl, her prayers would be about getting a new dress or hair band, as though God were a big gift machine. As she grew older, I tried to teach her that praying is an expression of our faith in God. In other words, we believe and trust that God's goodness will be granted to us through prayer, even when the immediate answers are "no" or "not yet." This is part of the human agony of prayer. The waiting (as we know all too well!) is the hardest part.

We further recognize that God is not a cosmic, divine Amazon.com. God does not answer all prayers the way we want. As Jesus faced his death, he prayed in the Garden for "this cup [of suffering to] be removed." God did not remove it. However, Jesus continued faithfully to follow God's will. Even as we face death in our family, we pray that death will pass by our family member, but this does not always happen. Eventually, death comes to us all.

Therefore, prayer involves trust. When Jesus tells us to ask, knock, and see, he is speaking more about our trusting God rather than about our receiving things from God. We need to trust God and try to discern God's will. Trust God in times of pain. Trust God in times of death. As our trust in God deepens, our prayers begin to change. We become the children who will pray the prayer that gives us some peace and understanding. Prayer leads us to the mystery of God and we cannot fully understand God's being, will, actions, and mercy towards us. Prayer can help us even in times of death.

We all face death, our own and that of others. As I look back upon the death of my mother, I wonder if rather than praying for God to spare my mother, perhaps I should have prayed as my seminary classmate did when she was diagnosed with cancer. She prayed, "Yes, why not me?" Her response to cancer shocked me. I was surprised she could pray with such acceptance, rather than crying out to God in despair. She accepted her cancer with grace and trust in God. In so doing, she found peace. Remembering my friend's words, my own prayers for my mother soon became a prayer of thanksgiving for the promise of eternal life in the end times. There is mystery in prayer. At the end of our journey of life, we fall before the face of God in awe of the mystery in the fullness of God's compassion, mercy and grace.

This passage from Luke's Gospel reminded me that we are not to give up on prayer but to pray without ceasing. We acknowledge God's mercy and pray in all the circumstances we face. In prayer, what we are truly seeking, whether we know it or not, is God. For it is through prayer that we recognize God's grace towards us which sustains us even as we walk through the shadowed valley of death. We pray so that we might know, trust, and live with and for God.

As a parent, it is important that I teach my children what it means to pray. That God is not a "divine Santa Claus" but someone who listens to us and wants to be in relationship with us. We need to pray without ceasing. I try to tell my girl to pray all day long. At school, at home, or wherever she may be. This is hard to teach, let alone live by.

Prayer is difficult. It is a discipline brought forth from faith, hope and trust.

Reflections:

1. My mother taught me to pray in all circumstances. How do we pray in our pain and struggles?

2. What does it mean to be in communion with God when we feel that God is so far away? How do we draw closer to God so that we can feel the presence of God in our daily lives and in times of death and sorrow?

3. What drives you to overcome difficulties, particularly the

ones that threaten to overtake you? How do you overcome hopelessness?

4. Losing my grandmother was the hardest thing in my life. How do you deal with loss? How do you mourn and overcome sorrow? How do you pray in times of loss and death?

5. Life can dish out terrible experiences of tragedies. To overcome tragedies, we turn to God for healing. How do you handle tragedies?

6. What has been the most difficult event in your life? How do you inch yourself away from death, sorrow, pain, and towards healing?

Chapter Four

Rehearsals in Life

"Rehearsals"
Elisabeth Sophia Lee

"But I trusted in your steadfast love; my heart shall rejoice in your salvation. I will sing to the Lord, because he has dealt bountifully with me."

- PSALM 13:5-6

When the Nutcracker production ends in December, I get about three weeks of relaxation with no dance. I chill out and try to forget about my sore feet and back. During Christmas break, I spend a lot of the time resting in bed, but I also try to remain active by jogging, stretching, and doing aerobics so I don't lose my flexibility. Regardless, after the break, it is hard for me to get back into the routine of going to dance classes four or more times a week.

I recently started classes again and have been really sore. Dancing after a long break is hard on a dancer's body, especially when I'm not assiduous about stretching and conditioning my muscles. So going to dance was a huge switch. As a result, I'm suffering from foot aches and sore muscles. I push through them. I am used to pushing myself. During rehearsals, although I am constantly sore or hurt, I am always determined to keep going.

This week was observation week at ballet, so my family was allowed to come and watch me. I was very nervous to dance in front of them. So I try to discourage my family from coming. It is usually only my mom who observes but I really don't like it. Every observation week I tell her not to come. But without fail, she always comes to see me dance.

I actually find it easier to dance in front of strangers than people I know. If I make a mistake in front of strangers, they will not remember me, so it's okay. On the other hand, I feel if I make a mistake in front of my family, they will remember it forever. Still, in my nervousness, I danced for my mom. She enjoyed my dancing and was very impressed, although I think every mom is impressed with her children. She took some pictures and videos of me and wanted to post them on social media.

I am so happy God has given me a talent for dancing. I am lucky to be gifted with something that many girls dream of having. I love using the movement of my body to make others feel happy. My movement becomes an extension of my praise and love for God. Even King David danced before the Lord (2 Samuel 6:14). My mom thinks it is a gift from God to be able to dance. She always complains that she is not a good dancer and wishes she had been able to take dance lessons when she was younger, but she never had the money to take any private lessons. I am so grateful I have been given the opportunity.

I realize many are not as privileged as I am. My mom often talks to me about seeing so many poor people living on the streets and begging for their food in Haiti and India. Since I have a home and my mother is able to pay for my dance lessons, I feel grateful and happy that I have these opportunities to learn to dance.

I am quite young right now and I feel I don't have the talent or gifts to help feed the poor like Jesus taught us. I do hope that through my dancing, and eventually through some other ways, I can do something to help feed the poor and make people happier. I would like to offer free dance workshops to help those who cannot afford to take private dance lessons. I also hope that my dance performances can brighten up people's lives as I try to bring more beauty into the world through my performances.

"Palm Sunday Ponderings: Jesus and Those in Need"
Grace Ji-Sun Kim

"The crowds that went ahead of him and that followed were shouting, "Hosanna to the Son of David! Blessed is the one who comes in the name of the Lord! Hosanna in the highest heaven!"

- MATTHEW 21:9

Palm Sunday is the day when Jesus entered Jerusalem and the crowd cheered. The people yearned for a leader to help create a new kin-dom of God for the Israelites who had been subjected to one empire or another for the better part of six hundred years. As he rode into Jerusalem, the crowd greeted Jesus as the one who would fulfill their desires. It was a moment of triumph.

Many Christians continue to have similar expectations of Jesus. They focus on Jesus as a triumphant figure, a powerful Jesus who can come into our lives and make a triumphal change. His return is embedded in the Nicene Creed which Christians around the world recite every Sunday: "from thence he shall come again, with glory, to judge the quick and the dead."

A few summers ago our family visited the Vatican Museum and the Sistine Chapel. It was a very hot day. My children were complaining about walking around the Vatican. It was hot, muggy and overcrowded. It was a miracle that I didn't lose any of my children in that big crowd of tourists all walking around and admiring the artwork. After much complaining, we finally found our way inside the Sistine Chapel. As we entered, we were totally awestruck by Michelangelo's masterpiece painting on the ceiling. My children who had been complaining the entire time we were in the Vatican Museum finally stopped complaining and they were amazed at the beauty of the room and the painting on the marvelous ceiling. My girl held my hand and couldn't believe that we were in one of the most beautiful buildings that we had ever entered.

As we toured the rest of the chapel, I realized that much of the art portrayed a triumphant Jesus. The sculptures showed a powerful Jesus who is strong, muscular and almighty. The paintings depicted a majestic savior enthroned with angels all around him. Within "traditional" church and Christianity, many find comfort in depicting a powerful Jesus.

However, this is only one side of Jesus and one dimension of God. This may be what Luther called the theology of glory — Jesus represented as we humans like to see him. If we only focus on this side, we fail to see the Jesus of the gospels who taught at length on how we are to live and to concentrate on the lesson of the cross. If we continue to focus on a triumphant, powerful Jesus, we see only the human constructions of Jesus becoming Christ and we fail to recognize the humanity of Jesus and the meaning of his sacrifice. We will forget that Jesus wept at the death of his friend Lazarus (John 11:35), and that Jesus prayed before his impending arrest and execution, "Father, if you are willing, take this cup from me; yet not my will, but yours be done" (Luke 22:42). We need to recognize the other side of Jesus who proclaimed his mission in the words Jesus read of the prophet Isaiah, "The Spirit of the Lord is on me, because he has anointed me to proclaim good news to the poor. He has sent me to proclaim freedom for the prisoners and recovery of sight for the blind, to set the oppressed free" (Luke 4:18).

Jesus loves those who are the forsaken people. And Jesus wants us to do the same: feed the poor, care for our sisters and brothers who are sick, and visit our brothers and sisters in prison. This is part of life. How we go through different rehearsals in life, this is something which we need to be practicing and trying to do every day. This is something which I try to teach my children.

Despite these and other examples, Christians often want to ignore or push aside the humanity of Jesus who cared for the poor. Instead we emphasize the triumphant Jesus of the Renaissance and Baroque European paintings, stained glass windows, frescos, and music. Jesus loved the poor and was "the poor." Jesus was born poor, lived poor, and died poor. Jesus has shown us how we are to live out our life. This is the life rehearsal that we need to engage in and try to live out.

I often tell my daughter that our life rehearsal is much like her ballet rehearsals. We need to rehearse aspects of life over and over again so that it becomes natural. Jesus asked us to love the poor and be with the poor. This is something that we need to do continuously so that it becomes a natural act. Jesus showed us how we are to live; we need to follow.

In our society, we know who these "poor" people are. We know the ones who are lost, forgotten, or in prison. One person who keeps tugging at my heart is the Korean American missionary, Kenneth Bae, who was in prison in North Korea. He has been charged and found guilty by the North Korean government of trying to overthrow that regime. He was sentenced to fifteen years of hard labor in prison. Kenneth Bae is a father, a husband, a son, and a brother. He was finally released on Saturday, November 8, 2014 along with fellow American Matthew Todd Miller. Like every other person, they are humans whose lives are worth fighting for. We also need to take care of those who are cast out and on the margins, such as the LBGTQ community, people of color, and those who are wasting away in our prison systems.

Jesus cared for people neglected or discarded by the powers and customs of his day, and those who suffered from leprosy. He crossed religiously and culturally established lines to welcome and to love in practical, caring ways that transformed lives and challenged the status quo. Jesus invites us to do the same — to remember we are all God's beloved children and to treat all people as our brothers and sisters, particularly those in need or on the "outside." This needs to be our practice in life and should be our life rehearsal. We need to remember and live Jesus's words, "I tell you the truth, whatever you did for one of the least of these of these brothers [and sisters] of mine, you did for me" (Matthew 25:40).

Reflections:

1. Life is a series of rehearsals. For what in life are you rehearsing? Is it to bring more joy, justice, and love into the world, or for some other reason?

2. What gifts has God given you? Can you use these talents to benefit the community or help those in who are in need of some kind?

3. How are you following the commandments of God to be with the poor? How can you live out the words of Matthew 25:40?

Chapter Five

Being Grateful

"Being Thankful for What We Have"
Elisabeth Sophia Lee

"It is good to give thanks to the Lord, to sing praises to your name, O Most High."

- PSALM 92:1

We celebrated my brother Joshua's eleventh birthday with my mom's best friend from High School, Janice. My older brother wanted hamburgers and pizza. My mom and I wanted Chinese food. We like restaurant dishes that are hard to make at home! So, when we arrived at the Chinese restaurant, my brother became annoyed and grumpy. I didn't understand what he found so wrong with eating Chinese food, so I ignored him. Problem is, my mother is never happy when I ignore my brother.

This is one of the difficult things about having two brothers. I would much rather have a sister with whom I share my deepest secrets and with whom I can share my clothes and style our hair together. I wish I had a sister. I look at my mom and my aunt's relationship and wish I had a sister, too.

My mother tells me that when I was little (3.5 years old) and fought with my younger brother, I would yell out, "I didn't want a brother, I wanted a sister!" No such luck.

Anyhow, I guess life isn't always about getting what

I want. There are a plenty of things that I ask for from my mother, and she rarely gets me what I want. I admit, I sometimes get upset about that, but then I try to forget about it and move on.

To be honest, when I ask my mother for more clothes, I know that I don't really need more. It is just that I want the latest fashion. As I grow, I need to learn not to allow the passion for possessions take over my life. My mother has told me many times of the unfortunate people around the world. In fact, I have witnessed it in my own travels with my mother. Together we went to Brazil and to Myanmar and I have seen people living in total poverty. So, even as I struggle with wanting more things to make my life more 'enjoyable,' in the back of my mind I know there are poor children all around the world who have less than I can ever imagine. I know that I am supposed to give thanks and be grateful for everything that I have.

My challenge is to be grateful for the things that I have— a warm house, a beautiful bedroom, wonderful friends and for my family…and even for my two brothers.

"Writing and the Community that Sustains Me"
Grace Ji-Sun Kim

"Surely God is my help; the Lord is the one who sustains me."

-PSALM 54:4

Writing is difficult for me. Some days when I try to write, nothing comes. I spend hours surfing the Internet. I stare mindlessly at my laptop and drift off into Neverland. Some days when I am not motivated, I go to Twitter and read "The Tweet of God" which always gives me something to laugh about. Some of my more recent favorite tweets are these: "Sometimes, if you believe in something hard enough and deeply enough, nothing happens," and "I need to be praised and acknowledged constantly because although I am omnipotent I am extremely insecure." Very funny.

I also like to read tweets by Anne Lamott, a talented writer and teacher. Her books seem to be written effortlessly and her thoughts touch our hearts – as if she knows each one of us individually. It is a real talent to challenge and motivate others to grow into their better selves the way she does.

I love her writing and highly respect her openness about life. She freely shows her vulnerability and frustrations about being a professional writer. In her book, *Bird by Bird*, she shared some of her personal struggles of writing and being a writer. She thought that she would be a famous writer and realized that people didn't even recognize her. Some of her tweets describe the difficult life of writing various drafts and editing her own work. These reveal her own hurdles as she produces another book. "Here is what writing is about. One: Go over and over the same sentences and phrases, until they are not as bad and fraudulent as they were before," and "Day 1 on new shitty 1st draft is stepping into a cold lake, in an old swim suit, hand in hand with a dentist who wants a peek at your gums." Ouch.

Lamott's tweets allow me to see her 'writing in progress' as well as the final product. The writing in progress is the painstaking work it takes to craft a phrase or sentence. Even professional writers have difficulty writing. Bringing clarity to a morass of ideas doesn't come easily. I always tell my daughter the most worthwhile things in life are difficult to accomplish. Writing is one of them. She has come to realize that as we've co-written this book.

Lamott's openness assures me that we all belong to this human race and that each of us has our own set of problems and difficulties in our journey in life. As we journey together, we can take comfort in knowing that even those whom we idolize have difficult days.

Whenever we are reminded that no one is immune to difficulties, we find comfort. "This is life," as they say. During the challenging times, we hold onto our faith more tightly and lean on our community of friends and family. Women's communities have sustained many people during times of loneliness, separation, loss, and death. When I look back at my own life journey, I recognize that it is the feminist network of communities and friends that have sustained and nurtured me over the years and through the challenges. They have comforted and encouraged me to stay strong and even rejoice in my failures. I will always be thankful for them. Having a sense of gratefulness in our heart lifts us up and carries us even further. It strengthens us and pushes us forward. Though the sun sets, it always rises again.

Reflections:

1. What do you desire to have the most in this world? What is driving this desire? Do you need the things that you desire?

2. Some of our desires are driven by advertisement. They make us feel we need those things. How do you temper media's influence on you?

3. Make a list of some of the things for which you are grateful. How can you make this list longer?

4. What practices of gratitude do you have?

5. What sustains you when you are down? During those low points, for what are you still grateful?

6. How do you sustain others? How could you sustain others?

7. What is the role of your faith community when it comes to helping you flourish during life's struggles and hardships? How has this community made you more grateful for the things you have?

Conclusion: Family

We are all part of a family. It may be through biology, adoption, surrogacy, marriage, or even by choice. Regardless, we all belong somewhere, even if it is as described in Kurt Vonnegut's Cat's Cradle, an ad hoc karass. In the familial institution, there will be undeniable uncertainties, as some are happy and others struggle just to stay in their own community of origin.

As we go through life with siblings, parents, aunts, uncles and grandchildren, there are obstacles that may hinder us from growing and developing further in our lives. Inevitably, there are times when we will take two steps forward and one step back. During hardships we try to build stronger families able to sustain us and encourage us to confront the storms. However, as we progress through different stages in life we establish other communities outside of the familial unit, and these serve as sources of love, connection, and hope.

Regardless of our respective family and community, it is imperative that we bring our best to them. We learn how to honor our elders and make our personal life a dress rehearsal for the real thing — a kin-dom of God here on earth. We practice being grateful for everything that we have for we do not know when death will come knocking on our door or call for those who we love. We get in the habit of not taking the present for granted, and of showing our appreciation to all those whom we love now, regardless of the unknown tomorrow.

Life Happens

Chapter Six

Discrimination and Racism

"Racism in Everyday Events"
Elisabeth Sophia Lee

"There is no longer Jew or Greek, there is no longer slave or free, there is no longer male and female; for all of you are one in Christ Jesus."

- GALATIANS 3:28

We moved from Canada to the United States in 2004. It was a big move for us, leaving one country and creating a home in a new country. I love shopping, and because the move involved getting rid of our old stuff and buying new things for our new house, that made the move more fun for me! Therefore, when my mother said one day that she wanted to go to the department store to shop for a new clothes dryer, you can imagine it was wildly exciting for me.

I was only five years old at the time, but I still remember being thrilled about going to the big department store. Once there, my two brothers and I stayed busy trying to keep up with my mom who went from one end of the store to the other looking at everything but a dryer. When we finally made it to the dryers, my mother talked with a sales representative about all of the different kinds, and my brothers and I checked out the different colors and styles of washing machines on display. Three male department store representatives approached us and, leaning close, one of them said to me, "Hi little girl. *Ching Chong, Ching*

Chong."

My mother was near enough to see and hear what was going on. I was a little confused by the racially demeaning remark, and from the expression on my mother's face, I knew what had just happened was definitely not good. She quickly came to where I was standing and said something to the man who then left, along with his colleagues. My mother reported the interaction to another sales representative and to the store manager.

This event has become etched in my memory. At the time, I was not sure what the comment meant. But as I grew older, I learned how racially demeaning his comment had been. Particularly looking back on the event now, I can't believe that the other workers smirked and laughed while the speaker diminished me.

This unexpected encounter made me realize racism is prevalent and can be experienced in any circumstance. Racism is not simply something that adults like my mother theorize about in books. It is a living reality for many people. When I go to school, I experience racism. When I go shopping, I feel racism. When I travel, I encounter racism. It's everywhere.

I have found it difficult to deal with racism, and it has not grown any easier with age. When I was five, my mother was there to intervene on my behalf. Now I have to learn to confront it myself and fight to eliminate it from our society. I have learned in church that God loves everyone equally and that we are to treat others in this same generous way. Though we are different in certain particulars, the only peaceful way forward for me and my generation is to live out such love day by day.

"Back to School:
What Are We Teaching our Children?"
Grace Ji-Sun Kim

"The second is this 'you shall love your neighbor as yourself.' There is no other commandment greater than these."

- MARK 12:31

When my three children go back to school in late August, I can't get the song, "It's the Most Wonderful Time of the Year" out of my head, and it isn't even Christmastime!

My children spend a lot of the summer at home (when we are not traveling), so it is always a wonderful feeling to have them out of the house and back to school. I start – in June – counting the weeks, days, and hours before my children return to school!

Like many parents in the United States, I keep my children busy throughout the year. They belong to sports teams, go to music lessons, attend Korean language school, and engage in other extra-curricular activities. I sign them up for as many things as I can afford, while also allotting for time to drive them back and forth. This inevitably adds up to a lot of activities, a lot of driving, and considerable expense.

Sometimes it feels like the children are running from one activity to the next. At one point, things got so busy my eight-year-old son asked, after he returned from a hard day at school, "Why did you have to sign me up for school, too?" That's a busy kid.

We know school is not optional for children. They

must attend school and try to receive the best possible education. However, when I examine some of the traditional curricula of elementary schools, I find that important topics are missing. Courses in history and literature could teach relevant topics such as the nature of racism, sexism, and privilege. Books that quickly come to mind as resources, suitable for fifth and sixth grade, might be *Huckleberry Finn, Oliver Twist,* or *To Kill a Mockingbird.* Racism, sexism, and privilege are all woven into the social fabric of our society, and these three novels indicate that the problems are chronic. It is important for children to understand these issues and how we should work to live in peace and good faith with one another.

Racism remains a problem in North American society. It promotes domination of the weak by a privileged group in the economic, social, cultural, and intellectual spheres. Racism is so embedded in our society that when laws finally ban it, it mutates, like a virus, into forms with hidden symptoms, harder to demonstrate in courts. Racism appears as jokes, like when Chris Rock joked about the three Asian American children that he brought onto the stage at the Oscars 2016. He joked that kids like them made phones, inferring child labor. He also made stereotyped jokes about these Asian children, as if it is alright to be racist as long as you are funny.

As long as parents neglect to teach children about racism, it will be sanctioned in the minds of those who inherit the power of the vote and the power of the dollar. It will also break out as a rash in unexpected times and places, a testament of this being the murder of nine people at Charleston's Emanuel African Methodist Episcopal Church on June 17, 2015.

I am haunted by the racism and discrimination I experienced in my own childhood – it has been like a thorn in my side throughout my life. I still remember being taunted for being Asian. I remember all the racial slurs in the school playground. "*Ching Chong, Ching Chong.*" Yes, the same words as were said to my daughter years later in that department store. It was painful. As a child, it was a pain that I never talked about with my other Asian friends nor my family. Growing up in an Asian culture of honor and shame, it is too shameful to talk about such pain. It is shameful to discuss how others are making fun of us as Asian Americans. There was no place to share my deep sorrow and dismay, and these experiences drove my melancholy heart to despair.

Now, as an adult, I feel it necessary to share my experiences of racism so that we can overcome it. My experiences have been a way to start teaching my children about racism. I continue to struggle with this subject, especially as it pertains to my daughter, since racism and sexism are often intertwined. My children share with me their experiences of racism, and I hope that instead of being discouraged by it, they will overcome it. Living with this deep pain definitely contributed to the intense anger I felt when I saw the sales associate make a racial slur about my daughter. At first I froze, watching in disbelief, transported back in time to my childhood experiences of racism, which were so painful I tried desperately to ignore their existence. But my girl's incident opened the floodgates of painful emotions all over again. I didn't expect my own children to go through the same horrors I had experienced as a child. I thought that the world had moved on. I thought we were in a better world. In a moment, that notion was shattered. I felt compelled to look the three sales associates in the eye. I gave them a frightful stare as they stood in shame of what they had done to my child.

As an Asian American woman, I often experience

racism and I attempt to unmask it, to reveal it as the anti-Christian reality it is. Racism alienates people from the dominant culture. Asian Americans are constrained by an invisible boundary which has prevented us from belonging to the mainstream culture at work, school, and in the broader community. This has held true in my own struggle for justice and parity, and it will remain true as long as a "dominant race" maintains the ability to hire, promote, and measure ability. Therefore, it is necessary that we all work together to remove these barriers by equalizing power among all members of society. We should not be judged by the color of our skin but by our character and our actions.

Racism leads the dominant culture to marginalize people who do not conform to the culture's standard. Often this standard is arbitrary, with no basis in substantial matters, such as when women are excluded from some aspects of church, because men have inferred that it is only males who can hold power. because Jesus was male. Jesus himself never excluded women or children. Only disciples of Paul, it seems, lowered the status of women. Racism and other "isms" drive people to the margins of culture and society. People on the margins live in between places. Immigrants neither belong to their native culture nor to their host culture: they dwell in two places at once. Marginality reinforces the inclination to stay in a ghetto or segregated society. This, in turn, creates feelings of hopelessness, pain, and subordination as people who have been marginalized are trapped between remaining safely behind those barriers and attempting to progress past them.

If racism goes unchecked or unchallenged, it will continue to perpetuate prejudice, discrimination, white privilege, and white supremacy. This has monumentally negative effects on all of society. We need to talk about this with our children from an early age, so that they understand it and feel empowered to tackle and overcome this barrier in society. They need heroes and models who look like them, and they need to see them from the very beginning of life. Children must develop their own pride, and understand the ways in which the acid of racism erodes that pride. Many racial/ethnic groups, like the Irish, Italians, and African-Americans, have nationally recognized cultural heroes. Our work is to expand that to include all racial/ethnic groups.

In addition to recognizing heroes from all the cultures that make up the United States, we can expand the traditional curricula of elementary schools. The earlier we start adding these important matters to our school curriculum, the better a society we can build. The better the society we can build, the closer we come to welcoming the reign of God in this world. Together let us envision and create a world that accepts all people as made in the image of God, regardless of race, ethnicity, and gender.

Reflections:

1. When have you experienced discrimination or racism, either toward yourself or others? How did you handle the situation?

2. How can we counter racism, stereotyping, and discrimination?

3. In our homes, in our schools, and in our churches, how might we teach our children to love and accept people from all parts of the world instead of stereotyping them? What would such a world look like?

4. What do the gospels teach us about loving one another? Or about the reign of God?

5. How can we establish and live in a just and peaceful soci-

ety that reflects the Reign of God?

Chapter Seven

Strategies for Life

"Family Trips with an Agenda"
Elisabeth Sophia Lee

"'Honor your father and mother'—this is the first commandment with a promise: 'so that it may be well with you and you may live long on the earth.'"

- EPHESIANS 6:2-3

I never imagined our family would travel to Brazil. I imagined South America as a faraway land, with landscapes and territories different from anything I had ever seen. It seemed like a continent I would be able to visit only in my dreams or in a novel! So I was very excited when I learned that my family would be visiting Rio de Janeiro, Brazil.

Before we travel anywhere, my mother makes all of us do some homework. It is never a 'free' trip, but always something we have to work for. My mom always says, "There is no such thing as a free lunch." She asks us to research the country and city we are visiting, and to write a story and a reflection about where we are going, with a list of places we want to visit and things we want to do. During the trip, we each keep a journal to discuss and reflect on the places we have visited. She also expects us to write a blog after the trip, which she posts on her personal website. It has become a routine. It is what we do.

However, as I reflect upon this routine, I realize that

none of my friends have to do all of this work when they go on a trip. Our routine has something to do with my mother's idea of "learning while playing." I admit that all of this writing about my travels has improved how I write. I don't always enjoy it, but my mother keeps telling me it's a good thing and that I'll look back at my journals and have fond memories of my childhood and all the different places I visited.

The fact that my mother always asks the best from us in all our school work, projects, and tests may be an Asian and Asian American expectation. She expects perfection or near perfection. This usually translates into getting an A in class. This is good, in some ways, as it pushes me to do my best. But, as you can imagine, it is also a source of stress. I do not see my non-Asian American friends having the same kind of pressure to excel in all they do in school. Their parents seem to be happy and satisfied they are "trying." As long as they "try," they are in good standing with their parents.

No wonder I sigh about what it means to be an Asian American girl with its cultural, religious, and philosophical expectations. Sometimes, I wish my parents were less Asian American. My friends' parents don't always ask what grade they got or how they rank relative to other kids in the class. Sometimes, it is embarrassing that my parents expect so much from my brothers and me. I often try to imagine what it would be like to grow up white rather than Asian American.

My mother tells me I should be happy and proud to be Asian American. She tells me how lucky I am compared to when she was growing up. She constantly reminds me that life is good and easy for me whereas her life was difficult due to a lack of resources, an inability to speak English, and other issues that I have not had to endure.

Well, no matter what, I am who I am. I'm glad I am an Asian American teenager who grew up with Asian American parents. Part of the Asian culture is to honor our elders and our ancestors. This goes along with the scriptural commandment of honoring our parents. The Ephesians passage reminds us that honoring our parents is one commandment with a promise. Part of honoring our parents is by obeying them.

When my parents ask me to write the journal, I try to honor them by obeying them. When they ask me to excel in my school work, I obey them so that I can honor them. The two are connected and interrelated. Additionally, I see my parents obeying their elders. My parents have set a good example for me and I am always thankful to them. My parents teach me the best they know how, the best ways to excel. For that, I am very lucky. I should be happy with my Asian American culture and try to do my best: not just to please my parents, but also to please myself. There is a personal reward for trying my best even if I don't get an A every time. The effort counts a lot.

I think good things come to those who honor their parents. The good part is, I did my homework. I wrote my blog. I did get to travel to Brazil. It was one of the most fascinating trips of my life!

"Redemption and Survival:
A Working Mother's Strategy"
Grace Ji-Sun Kim

"He is the source of your life in Christ Jesus, who became for us wisdom from God, and righteousness and sanctification, and redemption."

- 1 CORINTHIANS 1:30

Being a mother is one of life's busiest, fullest, and the happiest adventures. At the same time, it is the most challenging, crazy, and disappointing role one can have. Some women in the news make motherhood seem easy, such as Marissa Mayer, CEO of Yahoo, who returned to work soon after giving birth to her first baby. Of course, we know she has hired help to make it all look so easy, unlike most of the rest of us with fewer means who hang on by our fingertips.

I remember giving birth to my firstborn. It was a hot August day and I was in pain for weeks after the delivery. The stitches fell out, my breasts were sore, and my body was stretched. I ached for so long I thought I would never recover. I could not believe other women returned to their routine so soon after birth. I looked at them and wondered, "What is wrong with me?"

Jump ahead eighteen years. I am now a working mother of three beloved children who keep me very busy. I sometimes fail to remember when their soccer games are scheduled or when their piano lessons occur during the week. Every week and every day is a challenge for me to survive as I juggle my work and the obligations of motherhood.

I am doing the best I can, and sometimes it doesn't feel as if it's enough. My daughter complains and tells me I am putting too much emphasis on life as a learning experience. I tell her everything in life is a learning experience. Whether it is good or bad, it is all a learning experience which will hopefully make us better. So, wherever we go, even to the grocery store, I tell my children to carry a book with them – just in case we get stuck in traffic and find that we have nothing to do.

When we travel, I make my children do research before we go and journal during and after our trips. I did this before our trip to Brazil, and my daughter was not fond of the research and writing exercise. She believed a trip is a time to relax and not do any work. I ignored her and told her that if she wanted to get on that plane, she'd better start reading and researching about Brazil! She did follow through on my request and obeyed me. I know that it isn't always easy for her to obey, but she does try her best.

So, in order to be successful in my own business and to raise half decent kids who will grow up to do something worthwhile with their lives, I try to implement some parental strategies. One of my survival strategies is to expend most of my energy on my oldest child and hope (with fingers crossed) that the habits I've inculcated in him will rub off on his younger siblings. I figure that if I instill good study habits in the oldest child, the two younger children will pick them up too. If the oldest develops the habit of daily music practice, the younger ones will too.

Some way or another, this method has worked for the past eighteen years. I am barely surviving with my work as I try to manage the livelihood of three young children. It is difficult to balance a teaching career with motherhood as both areas pull me away from each other.

Yet there are some downsides to this method. Potentially it puts a lot of pressure on the eldest child. And I tend to spend less money, energy, and time on the two younger children, and particularly hardly any at all on the youngest. He barely appears on my radar. I tell everyone that he gets away with everything simply because I'm not around to notice his faults or failures.

When all three children started school in August, it dawned on me that my two older children were very busy with their many extracurricular activities at school, while my youngest was involved only in choir. Once I noticed his lack of participation, I encouraged him to become more involved at school. He decided to run for vice-president of his class and eagerly prepared a short speech. His class thought his was the funniest. He ended his speech with "And this message is approved by Joshua Lee," to which the students responded with roars of laughter.

Joshua did not win. He did not seem particularly disappointed, yet trying to be a good mother, I kept assuring him that involvement was more important than winning.

Next day at school, he learned that the position of treasurer was open, and he decided to run for it. I strongly encouraged him to do so, reminding him that trying was more important than winning.

He came home with a huge smile on his face and the job of treasurer! I hugged him a thousand times, kissed him all over his face, and did a little dance with him. I was happy not so much because he won the election but because he would finally be doing more than just singing in the school choir.

I was truly proud of him. He learned that winning

isn't everything. And I felt redeemed as a working mother. For all the busyness that comes with work and raising children, little moments like these are a saving grace.

We get so busy that sometimes we forget these moments of grace. In these glimpses of grace, we see the redemptive power of Jesus in our lives. We are made righteous, sanctified and redeemed through the grace of Jesus. This is what saves us and allows us to "survive".

I know I will never be a "Marissa Mayer" who makes motherhood seem like an "un-interruption" to her life and career. But motherhood is an interruption and, in many ways, a good one.

Later that evening, my youngest son crawled into my bed to give me a goodnight hug. He talked a bit about his day at school and then asked, "By the way Mom, what is a treasurer?"

Gotta love him.

Reflections:

1. What are some struggles that you are facing as you grow up, perhaps with parents or siblings? What strategies have you come up with to overcome these struggles?

2. Different cultures enrich our world and our living. How have you come to appreciate your own unique culture? How do you learn about other cultures?

3. The Bible speaks about honoring our parents. How can we do this as children or young adults? In what ways is this or is this not a good strategy for life?

4. What are some of your strategies for surviving busy/ stressful times?

5. What are some of your biggest challenges in parenting? Where do you find encouragement or support for raising children? What sustains you?

6. Where and how do you experience redemption in motherhood?

Chapter Eight

Overcoming Our Fears

"Fearful"
Elisabeth Sophia Lee

"Be strong and bold. Have no fear or dread from them, for the Lord your God who goes with you; he will not fail you or forsake you."

- DEUTERONOMY 31:6

A few years ago, our family visited New Haven, Connecticut as my mother had a meeting there. We left early in the morning and drove for three hours to the gorgeous city. The ride felt short compared to our usual eight-hour drives to Toronto, Canada. When I travel, I am always impatient about how long it is taking us to reach our destination. I get very excited about arriving at the new city and seeing all the new wonderful things. Once I get to the new place, I am thrilled and want it to last forever. Unfortunately, I know that's not how the world works.

We arrived at the hotel and settled in the small room with two large beds. The room was small but it fit our needs. I immediately took a shower, but then regretted it because we decided to go to the outdoor pool for a swim. My mom's high school best friend, Janice met us at the hotel with her son, Edward. The pool was outdoors, so the water was slightly cold. Joshua, my brother, and Edward jumped right in. I am more cautious, and so took it one step at a time. As I was taking my time to get into the water, Joshua yelled, "Come on, face your fears!" My mom thought this was a hilarious and unusual thing for a ten-year-old boy to say to his older sister. She laughed about it with her friend for some time. When she laughs, sometimes, she cannot stop. Her laugh is very infectious, so I began laughing too, even though I didn't know what she was laughing about!

As he yelled it out, memories flashed about some fears I had already faced: singing a solo in front of a big crowd, competing in the Korean Language Speech competition for two years in a row (I won gold one year and silver the next), performing solos in my school musicals, and dancing as a lead in ballet performances. These events were things I overcame and got through without too much trouble. So I thought, swimming in cold water is nothing compared to those nerve-wracking encounters involving family, friends, or strangers. With that in mind, I jumped right in and overcame my fear. Yay!

When I look back on these events, I acknowledge that God was the one who enabled me to overcome some of my deepest fears. Whenever I am scared, I know God is with me and is encouraging me to break out of my comfort zone. God said God will always be with us, therefore I continue to trust God and believe God will be with me always and comfort me in all aspects of my life. God gave us the Holy Spirit and I believe the Holy Spirit will always strengthen me and help me face all my deepest fears. My mother has written several books on the Holy Spirit, and as she writes, she often talks to me about how the Holy Spirit works in our lives. It is still difficult for me to understand the Holy Spirit, but my mother continues to explain it and I try my best to grasp it. I trust that it will become clearer and clearer to me.

"Life's Cycle of Fear, Pain, and Suffering"
Grace Ji-Sun Kim

"The Lord is my light and my salvation; whom shall I fear? The Lord is the stronghold of my life; of whom shall I be afraid?"

- PSALM 27:1

March 18, 2014 marked the five hundredth day Korean-American Christian missionary Kenneth Bae had spent in a North Korean prison. Bae was arrested in November 2012 while leading a tourist group. North Korean state-run media alleges that he was attempting to lead a religious anti-North Korean religious coup. For that, he was sentenced to fifteen years of hard labor. Bae is a reminder to all of us that Korea remains divided. Brothers and sisters are separated and friends are divided by the demilitarized zone along the 38th parallel.

I was born in Seoul, South Korea. My mother and father were children during the Korean War, and my mother told me stories of how they had to flee during the war. She was a young child, one of eight. My grandmother gathered her eight children and walked for miles and miles to southern Korea. As they were fleeing one day, someone shot a bullet through my grandmother's thigh causing permanent damage to her leg. As a young child, I thought it was a wonderful war story of heroism and courage. I didn't realize then the agony, fear, and suffering my parents and my grandparents went through to stay safe and stay alive.

The Korean War ended with an armistice, and division of Korea at the 38th parallel. That division is a stark reminder of how a beautiful, lovely country can be separated and become filled with pain, sorrow, animosity, and suffering. The 38th parallel has kept family members and loved ones apart for over sixty years. Many divided families are unable to reunite or even to know whether their relatives are still alive and well. The heartbreak of living apart in their own country has brought lots of anger, tension, loss, and suffering. In Korea, people have a term for such suffering: *Han*. *Han* is a difficult word to translate into the English language. The closest way to describe it may be as 'unjust suffering' or a 'piercing of the heart.'

Koreans have experienced tremendous *han* over the last several centuries. As a small peninsula, their country was frequently invaded, either by Japan or by China. Imperialist and colonialist subjugation has caused Korea enormous unjust suffering, including loss of culture, language and religion. Pain and unjust suffering left unaddressed is self-perpetuating. People will react or take revenge rather than address the pain. Therefore, it is important to break this cycle. *Han* causes fear. It sometimes prevents us from acting or living out our dreams.

Recalling my youngest child screaming, "face your fears" to his sister as he jumped into the icy cold pool while she tiptoed her way in reminded me of the pain I and others experience. In our pain, we want to hide or retreat. We want to run away from our fears, afraid they will be too painful to face.

It pains me to think about all of the fear in the world. Some have fear due to their Christian beliefs. When I was sixteen years old, I went on a short term mission trip with my church to Haiti. It was a wonderful opportunity to learn another culture and share the gospel message in a different country. I remember before the trip I learned that many Haitians might not welcome our trip. Some Haitians are suspicious of Christian groups — for good reason. So while I was there, I was always a bit afraid of what may happen to me.

One evening around 10 pm, I was hanging out with my youth pastor and friend outside the church building. I was sitting on a stone fence while the two were standing in front of me. It was quite dark and it was hard to see without the city lights to which I am accustomed. In the dark, all of a sudden, we heard a loud noise and I felt that someone had grabbed my legs. I screamed really loudly. Then I started to freak out and got scared that perhaps someone was trying to take me away. As the noise subsided, I became calm and tried to rely on God's promise of grace and that I did not have to fear.

There are some who fear seeking women's rights, and some who fear death or rape in war torn areas. Fear is real. Fear may paralyze us. It may subsequently destroy our lives. Perhaps rather than allowing fear to destroy our lives, we can take steps to overcome our fears. As we work towards overcoming our fears, we recognize that God is with us always. Furthermore, we face our fears because we recognize God is always with us.

Using the word *han* in our theological discourse has marked a welcome shift from focusing on our relationship with God to the relationships we have with our brothers and sisters, neighbors and strangers, and ourselves. When we cause others *han*, we are sinning against them.

The case of Kenneth Bae reminds me of the urgency for reconciliation, for breaking the cycle of fear, anger, and *han*. If the U.S. or South Korea retaliate for the wrongful imprisonment of an Asian American like Bae, it is not unlikely that North Korea will start a war. Bae's case reminds us of the need to work towards peace to break the cycle of anger and *han*, and to replace it with acts of liberty, justice, and reconciliation.

Reflections:

1. What are some of your greatest fears? What steps do you take to overcome them?

2. Trusting people is hard to do. Trusting God is also a challenge. How do you trust God?

3. How do you understand sin?

4. Have you experienced extreme unjust suffering/*han*? If you were able to overcome the damaging affects of *han*, how did you do so?

5. How do you help others out, especially those who are experiencing tremendous *han*?

6. What do you do to overcome injustice?

Chapter Nine

Making Mistakes

"Mistakes Happen"
Elisabeth Sophia Lee

"For God did not give us a spirit of cowardice but rather a spirit of power and of love and of self-control."

- 2 TIMOTHY 1:7

I am confident in myself.

Well... I usually am, anyway.

I have been dancing in the same production, The Nutcracker, for eight years and I know the production by heart. When I was eight my friends and family encouraged me to audition for The Nutcracker. I took their advice and have danced several different parts over the years. After rehearsals, I would come home and practice every step my teacher taught me. When I was not physically practicing the steps, I would rehearse them in my head. My mom encourages me to do this, so it has become routine now. It's particularly helpful because I've always been nervous about performing in front of people. I'm afraid of falling, tripping, or forgetting my next move.

The performance was drawing closer. Much as I wanted to, it was too late for me to back out of the performance. As I had on previous occasions, I shared my fears with my mom. She always tells me it is okay to make the mistakes, and that most of the time no one will know. I think she may be right; when I mention to my family and friends mistakes I've made in the past, I find that none of them had noticed.

On the day of my first performance, I was nervous. I stared at my reflection in the dance studio mirror, while my mom fixed my makeup. She had to make sure my eyes were done properly and my cheeks were pink enough. Then, I started curling my hair. I preheated the curling iron before wrapping strands of my hair around it. After a couple of seconds, I let the strands fall onto my shoulder, revealing a perfect, "bologna curl." I repeated the steps: "Gel. Curl. Spray. Hold. Gel. Curl. Spray. Hold." I did this over and over again until I had a full head of bouncy ringlets.

Once I was all made up, I began to review my dance steps to make sure I would not forget anything. This was what we dancers always do.

Every year, there are special memories or incidents. In 2013, there was a performance I would never forget.

I watched the girl who danced before me. She looked so majestic, flying in the air as her crown shimmered from the light reflecting off each gem. As I listened for my cue, my body started to tremble and I felt a little weak. I took my place in the farthest wing and was ready to fly onto the stage. I took a deep breath and then ran out.

I was in the middle of doing fouette turns, on pointe, when it happened. The thing I dreaded the most: I tripped.

I don't know how it happened, it just did. I could feel the heat rising to my cheeks as the music continued to play. I could hear the back stage crew gasp and my ballet teacher whisper it was "okay".

At first, I wasn't sure what to do. But then I remembered what my teacher told me: "*If you ever trip or fall on stage, don't come crying to me. Get up and keep dancing.*" So, that's exactly what I did.

I quickly got back into step as fast as I could. I also fought hard to hold back my tears. And, just like that, everything felt normal, like it had never happened. My smile reappeared as I finished my solo with an astonishing stance. *Yes, I did it!*

As I walked off stage, everyone congratulated me. It was the best feeling I've ever had. Later on, my family even surprised me with flowers and a card.

I thought to myself, "So what if I tripped? It isn't the end of the world. Mistakes happen."

That was a special lesson I learned. Sometimes, things happen which are beyond our control. Mistakes happen even after thousands of rehearsals. I cannot let something small, like a trip, get in my way. Whether in a dance performance or in other life circumstances, when I trip I just have to get up and keep going.

God does not just give up on us because we make a mistake. Even if we make a hundred mistakes, God does not give up on us. When we look at some of the biblical leaders God called, they were full of mistakes: Abraham, Jacob, Joseph, Moses, and David. God did not give up on them. In the same way, God will not give up on us.

"Investing in our Children's Future: Divestment, Sustainability, and Climate Justice"
Grace Ji-Sun Kim

"Yours, O Lord, are the greatness, the power, the glory, the victory, and the majesty; for all that is in the heavens and on the earth is yours; yours is the kingdom, O Lord, and you are exalted as head above all."

- 1 CHRONICLES 29:11

It was while my oldest son, Theo, was tagging along to Union Theological Seminary's recent "Religions for the Earth" and World Council of Churches' "Interfaith Summit on Climate Change" that he blurted out a question: "What has religion got to do with climate change?" to which I quickly responded, "Everything!"

My son's question continues to haunt me. Are many of our church members wondering the same thing? After all, many local churches are not addressing issues about the environment and climate change. Perhaps to them it feels like a scientific or a governmental issue and not something the church needs to tackle.

However, we are slowly seeing more and more religious organizations and church groups take climate change seriously. Local, national, and international churches and organizations now recognize that climate change and religion have everything to do with each other. Misinterpretations of scripture have contributed to the environmental crisis. Rather than understanding that human beings are co-creators with God, we have understood ourselves as ones who can dominate the earth. As a result, we have contributed to destructive climate change rather than to caring for the earth.

The September 2014 "People's Climate March" in New York was the world's largest march on that issue. Related events were held in 162 countries around the world and an interfaith service held on 21 September 2014 at the Cathedral of St. John the Divine. Part of the service involved an invocation for people of faith seeking to live justly and work towards sustainability.

Rev. Dr. Olav Fykse Tveit, the WCC General Secretary, has a great vision on how the World Council of Churches can continue to be a prophetic voice at the forefront of those working on our urgent topic of climate justice. Dr. Fykse Tveit challenged us with his words: "The interfaith movement is also a people's movement. Our 'Pilgrimage of Justice and Peace in the WCC' belongs to this people's movement, as we saw on the streets of New York and in many other cities of the world this weekend. We as churches are part of this people's movement. We will bring our specific contribution to this movement from our Christian faith perspective."

Climate change affects all people, but it especially endangers the lives of our sisters and brothers who live in poverty around the world. Because of this, climate justice is an economic, social, and political, as well as environmental issue. As Christians, if we are to respond faithfully to Jesus' command in Matthew 25:35, to feed the hungry, give drink to the thirsty, and offer hospitality to the stranger, then we must take climate change seriously. For it is the poor, the least of our brothers and sisters, who are most vulnerable to the repercussions of climate change.

The poor people who live near the shore or on islands are affected by storms. In many cases, they lose their homes, their livelihood and their families. When a mother survives a storm with her young kids, many find it difficult to rebuild their lives because of the lack of infrastructure. When they cannot find means of survival, some may resort to selling their children in human trafficking as their last resort of survival.

Jesus expects us to act. There are many things we can to do to help preserve the resources of the earth. We need to invest in ways that protect the earth and support sustainable development. We have to use renewable energy and divest from coal. We need to reduce consumption and work towards reusing and recycling.

The Reverend Henrik Grape, Officer of Sustainable Development at the Church of Sweden, believes that we cannot work towards climate justice while having investments pushing in the opposite direction. Therefore, faith communities must live out their words. His are not only words but "faith in action." For the Church of Sweden has divested itself of using fossil fuels. Other churches have done the same, like the United Church of Christ in the US and the Anglican Church in Aotearoa, New Zealand and Polynesia. At the global level, the World Council of Churches at its last Central Committee meeting, explicitly excluded fossil fuels from its investment portfolios. This request came from younger Central Committee members who, according to Dr. Guillermo Kerber, WCC Programme Executive for Care for Creation and Climate Justice, recognized the general ethical guidelines for investment that the WCC follows, but wanted to see fossil fuels explicitly mentioned.

Our actions, or lack of actions, will affect generations to come. But we must continue pushing the news of our agenda onto the public stage. Though over 300,000 people participated in the People's Climate March in New York City on 21 September (more than in the historic

1967 march against the Vietnam war in NYC), most major broadcast news stations did not feel the need to cover the historic march.

Maybe this is why my son and the younger generations do not see the relevance of religion to climate change. The mobilization of peoples, initiatives of religious denominations, and international organizations' efforts to care for creation and address climate change are rarely in the headlines. As a result, people fail to hear the urgent cry of religious communities to do something about the damage we are doing to this earth. As we learned in the early civil rights efforts, we need to make our own news.

Hopefully, assaults on the earth, the waters, and the sky will not be left for our children to fix. We have not picked ourselves up from our fall yet; that is our grave mistake. Just like my daughter who tripped in her dance recital, it is important to pick ourselves up and correct and learn from our mistakes. I realize that in the world of politics it is far, far more difficult to change direction, especially with such a large older population who grew up in an age of abundance, and so cannot see that it is in their interest to forgo that luxury. It is not too late to begin living sustainably and learning ways to do with less. I sincerely hope we can take steps to make a safer, cleaner, and more sustainable world for our children, in this our "borrowed" home. Our investments will affect our future. Let's invest in our children's future by creating a bright and clean world.

Reflections:

1. We make mistakes daily. Do you think you have learned from mistakes and have in turn influenced yourself for the better?

2. How do you move on from your mistakes?

3. Think of a couple of biblical characters who made mistakes. How did they rectify things and move on? Where is God's grace when we make mistakes?

4. We have made huge mistakes in how we care (or fail to care) for creation. In light of the environmental crisis, what are you personally doing to live for the next generation, for our children and their children?

5. What can your church do to save the planet?[1]

1 See Grace Ji-Sun Kim, "Mountain Top Experience and a Prophetic Call for Climate Change," *The Huffington Post*, November 23, 2014. Retrieved from: http://www.huffingtonpost.com/grace-jisun-kim/mountaintop-experience-an_b_5868524.html accessed Feb 7, 2017.

Chapter Ten

Rooting for the Underdog!

"The Underdog"
Elisabeth Sophia Lee

"For the Lord is good; his steadfast love endures forever, and his faithfulness to all generations."

- PSALM 100:5

My brothers and I recently watched France and Belgium compete in the FIFA World Cup. As I often do, I was rooting for the underdog, which in this case I felt was Belgium. It's a habit I come by honestly. My entire family does it. Whereas my dad roots for the underdog out of solidarity, my mother just likes to hear a 'Cinderella story,' when the weaker team fights and then pulls through to win.

There are great "underdog" stories in the Bible. For example, there was the famous story of David and Goliath. David was a young shepherd boy who had few warrior skills. He was not a fighter, just a boy who took care of the sheep. God had great expectations for this boy, who was the youngest son in the family. Somehow, he was chosen to fight Goliath, a giant Philistine whom no Israelite was willing to fight.

As I watched the FIFA World Cup and rooted for the underdog, I remembered I am the underdog in many situations. I am a minority student in my school, a girl, and the middle child. These are many things working against me! Yet, like David, I've learnt that if I trust God, God will help me. God will give me the strength to rise above the underdog role and become the strong one! If God is with me, whom should I fear?

This is something which has helped me as I go to school, dance, do community service and attend church. That I do not have to fear but can trust in God.

This is the faith story that should help us to prevail!

"Remembering Our Long Legacy and Contributions to America"
Grace Ji-Sun Kim

"There is no longer Jew or Greek, there is no longer slave or free, there is no longer male and female; for all of you are one in Christ Jesus."

- GALATIANS 3:28

Each year, May is celebrated as the Asian American and Pacific Islanders (AAPI) Heritage Month. The first celebration took place in 1977 and it was a ten-day celebration. It became a month-long celebration under George H. W. Bush in 1990. During this month, Asian Americans and Pacific Islanders remember our long legacy and contributions to the building of America. The White House Initiative on Asian Americans and Pacific Islanders has a blog focused on accomplishments and challenges. The theme for the month in 2014 was "I Am Beyond: Evoking the American Spirit". One post featured Julie Chu, four-time Olympic Medalist of the U.S. Women's Ice Hockey Team, Nina Davuluri, Miss America 2014, and Tina Tchen, Chief of Staff to First Lady Michelle Obama and Executive Director of the White House Council on Women and Girls all sharing their "I Am Beyond" Stories.

Asians have been migrating to all parts of the world, especially Europe, North America, South Africa, and Chile, since the early nineteenth century. Many migrated to the United States and Canada where Asians provided cheap labor. Asians first arrived in Hawaii and over 300,000 Asians entered the islands between 1850 and 1920. Asian labor became a commodity and the Chinese were among the first in that labor pool as they worked in the sugar industry in Hawaii.

The annexation of California in 1846 by the United States opened a door for Asian laborers to come to the mainland. Asians were not viewed as part of the human community, but as a disposable asset, where each one who falls is replaceable by a new Celestial.[1] No thought is given to the fallen individual. Chinese laborers were imported for the construction of the Transcontinental Railroad. Other Asians also arrived in response to the need for laborers to build America: the Japanese (1880s), Filipinos (1900), Koreans (1903), and East Indians (1907).

A desire for freedom often motivated Asian women's decision to immigrate. Other times men arranged the migration of Asian women – for profit and exploitation. Many women found themselves doing harsh work to feed, wash, and clean for the men. Many were not ready for the hardships of the immigrant life. Korean women worked long hours. Others who worked in the fields for wages spent a full day under the sun, perhaps with babies strapped to their backs, before returning home to fix dinner for their husbands or other male workers. Asian American women suffered in silence within a culture where their roles were defined by men.

In addition to this physically difficult life, Asian American women experienced psychological and legal suffering in the form of prejudice and discrimination. A series of restrictive laws against Asians was enacted, which severely limited their life within the United States. In 1870, Congress passed a law that made Asian immigrants the only racial group barred from United States citizenship. In 1882, the Chinese Exclusion Act suspended the immigration of Chinese laborers for ten years, but this was later

---

1 A common nineteenth-century term for the Chinese.

extended indefinitely, and lifted only in 1943. The 1917 Immigration Act further limited Asian immigration, banning immigration from all countries in the Asia-Pacific Triangle except for the Philippines, a U.S. territory at the time, and Japan. Japanese immigration, however, was subsequently limited by the 1924 Exclusionary Immigration Act, which stopped new immigration from Asia. In addition to these laws, Asians were segregated in public facilities and schools. They were subject to heavy taxation, prohibition of land ownership, and prohibition of intermarriage with whites. World War II brought the unfair internment of Japanese Americans. It was not until the passage of sweeping Civil Rights legislation in 1965 that state-supported discrimination ended.

These hardships are not well known within our society today. Their difficulties and experiences are overshadowed by the African-American experiences of racism. These difficulties continue today. Third, fourth, and fifth generations of Asian Americans living in the United States believe that they will never find 'home' in this land where they are viewed as the perpetual foreigner. In many ways, Asian Americans are the underdogs!

Racism against Asian Americans is disguised under different expressions like "model minority" or "honorific whites" within our society. This is evident in the recent scandalous life of Donald Sterling, Los Angeles real estate developer and NBA team owner, who favored Korean tenants over other minority tenants. Some people believe his preference shows he welcomes people of color; they do not recognize the racist undertones implied in such a preference of one group over another. We also see model minority effects in the hate crime killing of Vincent Chen in 1982. Society failed to recognize that Chen was targeted because he was an Asian American. He was being blamed for taking jobs away from "Americans." Although such targeting fits the definition of a hate crime, the perpetrators were not charged with the hate crime modifier.

Asian Americans make significant contributions to the growth of this country. They continue to play important roles in our life together. We have contributed culturally (for example: through tai chi, martial arts, tae kwon do, and the graphic arts). We have also contributed to the palette of America with sushi restaurants and Chinese restaurants, Asian food groceries, and Asian fruits and vegetables. We have added to the religious diversity through our Confucian, Buddhist, Taoist, Shinto, and Hindu religious heritage, and have contributed significantly in the areas of sports, academia, and technology.

As we embrace these joys and accomplishments, it is well to remember the suffering and pain so many Asian Americans endured to come to where we are today, in order that such atrocities are not repeated with, for example, the current distrust of Muslims. We need to do more. We need to promote more Asian Americans to the heads of companies and elect more Asian Americans to public office, even to the level of the president of the United States. We as Christians should be on the side of the Asian Americans and support them, as they are the underdogs.

The effort to eradicate racism from our society needs to involve more solidarity of the majority white Christians with their minority brothers and sisters, replacing charity and commiseration with empathy. We cannot continue to believe racism does not exist except when someone makes a racist remark. Racism is a disease like alcoholism. Lots of alcoholics don't drink, but that does not mean they are cured. Like alcoholism, racism can flare up at a moment's notice, erasing years of living in tolerance with other cultures. White privilege prevents many people from recognizing they perpetuate and contribute to racism. Therefore, we must ALL open ourselves and recognize that we need to work together to fight for social justice and liberation. Remaining silent on the sidelines is not an option in this matter. [2]

Reflections:

1. Who are the underdogs in your life? When were you an underdog? How did it feel?

2. How do you overcome being the underdog? How do you become the strong one who will overcome and beat the giant in your life?

3. How do you gain strength in your life? In what ways does your faith give you strength to overcome the giant?

4. How do you welcome the Asian American community into your own community? How does your church welcome those who are different? How do you cheer on the underdogs around you?

5. How do you counter racism? How are you building a more just society?

---

2 For further reading and discussion, please see Gary Y. Okihiro, *Margins and Mainstreams: Asian in American History and Culture,* (Seattle: University of Washington Press, 2014) & Seung Ai Yang, "Asian Americans," in *Handbook of U.S. Theologies of Liberation*, edited by Miguel A. De La Torre (St. Louis: Chalice Press, 2004), 173-184.

Church and Our Christian Faith

Chapter Eleven

Faith in Our World

"Love, Difference, and Myanmar"
Elisabeth Sophia Lee

"This is my commandment, that you love one another as I have loved you."

- JOHN 15:12

It was January 18, 2012 when my mother and I left for Myanmar (formally known as Burma), a country in Southeast Asia located between Thailand and India. Fortunately, I have had many such opportunities to travel around the world with my mother to her speaking engagements. I have traveled with her to Korea, Brazil, Canada, Mexico, Spain, Italy, France and across the U.S. But the trip to Myanmar was the farthest trip I had ever taken, and it would mean missing seven days of school. You know by now that my mother nonetheless made it an educational experience. As usual, she expected me to study the country and write some thoughts out before, during, and after the trip.

Thanks to studying the country's history, culture, and religion, already before we left on the trip, I had some notions of what to expect when I got to Myanmar. Even so, actually being there was an eye-opening experience because it was so different from home and from what I had expected.

We stayed at the "White Elephant Hotel" in Yangon (formerly Rangoon, the British capital of Burma), Myanmar. The term white elephant means "good luck" to the Burmese because they are extremely rare. My mother and I did end up seeing some white elephants at an exhibit, and I must say I was disappointed to find the elephants were a grayish-red color rather than the pure white color I had imagined.

In Yangon, my mother gave several lectures at the Myanmar Institute of Theology (MIT) and I had an opportunity to sing a cappella, "Morning Star, O Cheering Sight" before her lectures. It made me wonder whether my mother was nervous to give lectures at MIT, as I was truly petrified to sing a solo. Thankfully, I soon overcame this fear and enjoyed the chance to sing in front of the students.

In between my mom's lectures, we did some sightseeing. I had read about the beautiful pagodas, so I really wanted to see them. We talked to Burmese people and learned about their country and culture. Wonderful students from MIT guided us around the city. They did an exceptional job and I am especially grateful for their kindness as they also had classes to attend and homework to finish.

Through all our experiences, I was a bit taken aback that our hosts admired us for being Korean. Burmese people love Korean dramas, Korean movies, K-pop (Korean popular music), and Korean food. They were mesmerized by my mother's appearance and way of speaking. My mother and I giggled when everyone kept confusing her for a Korean actress who had come to Myanmar to give lectures. This trip was very special as I was welcomed into a whole different culture and world.

I had many new experiences during this trip. We saw many different pagodas (huge temples) and churches that were scattered across the city. Some pagodas were breathtaking with ornate decorations and intricacies. Each one was unique. Some of the pagodas were exquisitely decorated with gold and jewels. Lots of them had gems and gold hanging from the roofs which glittered in the sunlight. People brought donations of money, jewels, and gold to the pagodas to make the temples more beautiful and elaborate. The pagodas were filled with statues of Buddha. Some statues were so large that I simply could not comprehend how in the world they had been constructed and placed in the pagodas.

New to me also was the habit of taking off one's shoes before entering the sacred ground of the pagoda. Though in many Asian homes, everyone takes off their shoes, people rarely take off their shoes in public places. In our home, we do not wear shoes. So every time a friend comes over to visit, I have to remind them that we don't wear shoes in the house. However, when we go to our Korean American churches, we wear our shoes in the sanctuary.

In Yangon I tried many unfamiliar foods, including goat brain, along with many varieties of soups and fruits new to me. They were all interesting to taste! Familiar kimchi looked and tasted a bit different from the kind I eat at home and in Korean restaurants, but I enjoyed the novelty of it.

I quickly noticed that Burmese people are much more communally minded than we tend to be in the United States. It is a 'we' country and not an individualistic country. This is part of the Asian culture to think about the larger community of people rather than individual selves. They care about the community and try to help those in the community. The Buddhist temple takes offerings which are to be used to help the poor. Perhaps we can learn something from them about what it means to be in community. This is evident also in their (mainly Buddhist) religious heritage that emphasizes community rather than individualism and makes for a welcoming society, as exemplified by the students' hospitality toward us.

I do not know much about Buddhism, or about many other religions for that matter, but I do know we all need to get along. Whether we are Christian or Buddhist, we need to learn to live together. Many of my friends at school are Christian, but I also have Muslim and non-religious friends. No matter what their religion is, I get along with them all. Not getting along with people due to different beliefs or feelings of superiority is the cause of many cultural disagreements, armed conflicts, and terrorism.

I wonder why people of different faiths often dislike or distrust each other. Maybe it is because they don't like the other's ideas. Or perhaps they are afraid of the other. These differences are often lived out in land claims such as the Jewish claim to Palestine and the Indian claim to Kashmir. The Gospel of John tells us we are to love one another (John 14:12). I believe this includes everyone—Muslims, Christians, Buddhists, and non-believers. If we could only love by mandate, our world would be a more peaceful place. I wish that for my generation and for the ones to follow.

I have fond memories of my trip to Myanmar and am appreciative of everyone who helped us during our trip. I especially thank my mother. Without her, I wouldn't have been able to travel to Myanmar or the other wonderful places. I love her with all my heart for opening my mind to difference and for teaching me the power of love.

Christianity in a Global World
Grace Ji-Sun Kim

*"The alien who resides with you shall be to you as the citizen
among you; you shall love the alien as yourself, for you were
aliens in the land of Egypt: I am the Lord your God."*

- LEVITICUS 19:34

More than in previous generations, we experience a
world in which people of different ethnicities, religions, and
cultures live alongside one another. In this global neighbor-
hood, the probability of interacting with people from whom
we differ increases each year. In such a globalized and in-
ter-reliant world, interacting with one another intelligently
and with understanding is more important than ever if we
are to live in peace. So how do we welcome the stranger
into our communities, our churches, and our lives?

I traveled to Myanmar with my daughter to speak
at the Myanmar Institute of Theology. My daughter and I
enjoyed our time in Myanmar and have come to a deeper
understanding and appreciation of the Burmese people and
their multi-religious culture.

Yet in a city like Yangon in which we found a
breathtaking pagoda around each corner, I wondered, how
are Christians, Hindus, or Muslims supposed to survive
in such a Buddhist country? The President of Myanmar
Institute of Theology had invited me to preach at a Baptist
church. He said they had made several announcements
that I would preach. Since no government official objected
to my preaching, he believed it would be relatively safe. I
asked, "Safe?" He answered that in the past the threats of
violence had often been made against Christian preachers,
but that slowly the government and the community had

begun to open their eyes to Christianity. They recognized that it was a peaceful religion and was nonthreatening.

I didn't feel particularly reassured, but I preached anyway, and thankfully nothing unfortunate happened.

But it made me realize how crucial it is for us to learn to coexist with love rather than hatred. It is one reason I expose my children to people of different cultures, faiths, and traditions. Our trip to Myanmar I think made my daughter begin to realize that there is power and truth in our continuing to work in this way.

A few years ago, I attended a thought-provoking conference, "Understanding Religious Pluralism: Perspectives from Religious Studies and Theology" at Georgetown University. The gathering included scholars from many different religions who were teaching in different disciplines including religious studies, theology, ethics, Bible, and psychology. About one hundred twenty participants gathered to hear plenary speakers and panel presenters on religious pluralism.

I presented a paper "A Global Spirit" which was the basis of my book, *The Holy Spirit, Chi, and the Other*. It proposed that Christianity has no monopoly on the Spirit. We cannot say that the Spirit belongs only to Christians, thereby excluding people of different faiths who experience the Spirit in their lives and articulate the Spirit's work in their theology. Expanding our understanding of the Spirit will allow Christians to recognize how it exists in other religions.

All the conference papers generated challenging questions and discussions. I was particularly challenged by a quotation, read by a fellow panelist, from Henri Nouwen's book, *Reaching Out: The Three Movements of the Spiritual*

Life: "Hospitality, therefore, means primarily the creation of a free space where the stranger can enter and become a friend instead of an enemy. Hospitality is not to change people, but to offer them space where accommodation can take place." [1]

This speaks to many of the conflicts people face today. For example, there are so many conflicts fueled by disagreements over territory in Belgium, Ireland, Palestine, Tibet, Korea, and Kashmir, to name only a few countries. If borders were porous, would we fight less about land and borders?

When immigrants come to America to make it their home, we have the opportunity to respond with welcome and acceptance rather than the more familiar stances of hostility and racism that we tend to adopt particularly toward immigrant-foreigners who are not already a well-established part of the American mix. This generally means people who are not from the part of Europe that lies west of the Urals and north of the Mediterranean. Our fear and discomfort around people we experience as the "other" generates the difficulty of loving the neighbor and welcoming those who differ from us. Differences in language, food, dress, heritage, and religious beliefs become stumbling blocks.

We have a choice to make: Will we ignore or reject people from whom we differ, or will we welcome all God's children? Do we allow differences to separate us further? Or do we allow these differences to create spaces of opportunity where new friendships can grow and become a safe place of welcome? I hope that we will increasingly choose the latter and become a people to whom Jesus would say, "I was a stranger, and you welcomed me" (Matthew 25:35).

---

1 Henri Nouwen, Reaching Out: The Three Movements of the Spiritual Life (New York: Doubleday, 1986), 51.

Reflections:

1. What was a fun time you had with your parents or siblings that was also a learning experience? What made it a good time?

2. When have you experienced welcome? When have others welcomed you?

3. How do you welcome strangers? What can you do in your community to make it a place where strangers become neighbors and family?

4. How can we become a church of all nations?

5. How can we embrace our differences to live together in peace, harmony, and love?

Chapter Twelve

Saving the Earth

"Environmental Issues"
Elisabeth Sophia Lee

"Heavens and the heaven of heavens belong to the Lord your God, with the earth with all that is in it."

- DEUTERONOMY 10:14

I sometimes wonder how the world was created. How did God create all the birds, the trees, the flowers, the fish, and the insects? This world is a fabulously wonderful planet. It has everything to sustain, nourish, and generate life. Yet of all the things God created, human beings are the only creatures who are changing the planet's ecosystem for the worse, making the planet less habitable for everything and everyone. We are slowing destroying the very ecosystems that we need to sustain ourselves.

Taking care of our world is important for many reasons. The Earth is the only home we have, and if we neglect it, we can lose our ability to survive. It provides us with all our needs, such as food and water. But it is a finely balanced system, which operates on what cosmologists call The Goldilocks Principle. To endure, everything has to be "just right." Upset that balance, and there are deadly consequences. Earth is a living entity to be treated with respect and care.

Instead of doing unto the Earth as we would have

the Earth do unto us, we often treat the Earth as an other to be used at our convenience. Earth ensures our well being. And yet we repay her by polluting and exploiting her. A glance out our car windows at almost any roadside verge confirms this.

Our mother has long been drilling into us children the need to conserve and protect the Earth's resources. She constantly reminds my brothers and me to save water and energy –to turn lights off in rooms that we are not occupying, to take short showers (sometimes it seems as if she's telling us to get out before we've even started!), and to use air conditioning sparingly. We also drive a small, energy efficient car, use safe household cleaners that do not harm the environment, and avoid using insecticides and herbicides in our garden.

My mother reminds us to be cautious about what we put into the environment, to think of future generations, to remember that if we treat our planet well, we will create a sustainable future with clean water, clean air, clean soil, and fresh foods.

I often wish our house were solar powered, that we could reuse "grey" tap water to water our lawn and garden. I wish that the food, clothes, and other goods that we buy had less packaging. My mother talks about how as a child she used to take bottles to the store for re-use. Now we only do recycling, but still many people do not even do that, and just throw plastic bottles into the garbage. Our landfills are growing. They are filled with toxins which pollute the soil and the air.

How might we live our lives so that we do the least possible damage to our planet? Without change, we are well on our way to destroying our planet home.

"Our Disposable Lifestyle Accumulates Lots of Trash"
Grace Ji-Sun Kim

"In the beginning when God created the heavens and the earth, the earth was a formless void and darkness covered the face of the deep, while a wind from God swept over the face of the waters."

- GENESIS 1:1, 2

After we eat fast food, we throw away the cardboard pizza boxes, Styrofoam burger packaging, wax-coated drink cups, plastic utensils, and foil condiment containers. More often than not, we discard everything in which our food was served. What is worse, little of this is easily recyclable. Even when these items are produced using recycled materials, we throw them all away. That recycling centers often refuse cardboard pizza boxes because they invite mold when they are compacted may be a good argument for homemade pizza and homemade meals in general.

This disposable lifestyle has become convenient for us. As a result, many of us have lost our patience. We want meals that can be prepared with one push of a button on the microwave. We even get annoyed when the microwave, coffee maker, toaster oven or bread maker must be "programmed." We have learned that convenience is a priority and that we can live a disposable lifestyle.

As my daughter writes, I nag my children about such things often. Consequently, we mostly cook our own meals at home, buy fewer packaged meals, and make choices about eating, transportation, cleaning, and almost everything in life to minimize our impact on the Earth. And by

"Earth" I also include our air and waters, for now even our oceans are so filled with our plastic garbage that marine life is dying in droves from accidentally ingesting it.

Convenience comes with high costs to the environment now and for the generations to come. Americans generate 4.6 pounds of trash per person per day (and based on some information from my cat-loving friend, that goes up when a household has pets). That is twice as much trash per person as most major countries around the world. It has become easier and more economical to throw away broken TVs, radios, computers and furniture rather than repairing, refurbishing, or taking them to an electronics recycling facility. Recycled electronic waste is a valuable source of precious metals such as gold. A ton of electronic waste has fifty times more gold than a ton of gold ore dug from the earth.

This "disposable way of living" is creating huge amounts of damage to our land, as "disposable consumerism" has tripled waste in the U.S. since 1960. Of the garbage we produce, 32.5 percent is recycled or composted and 12.5 percent of waste is burned. This leaves 55 percent of our garbage filling landfills. The toxic chemicals from our garbage in landfills slowly filters into our neighborhoods through air, soil, and water.

The "disposable lifestyle" that we have adopted is contrary to the Genesis story of creation. We are no longer stewards of the good earth that God created. By our way of living, we are slowly destroying what is "good" in our world and bringing destruction and death to it.

What will stop us from harming the environment? What will jolt us into action? Would we act differently if there were no garbage trucks to remove our garbage from our sight or landfills into which to dump our "stuff"? Does

thinking about what we are bequeathing to future generations change what we do? As I think about the environmental crisis, all I can think about is what we are leaving
behind for our children. My daughter who suffers from a
lot of allergies will only suffer more with the rise of pollu-
tion. This is enough for me to want to change my ways and
live a "less disposable" lifestyle.

Reflections:

1. Taking care of the Earth is one of the most important
issues of our time. As young children and young adults, how
we can prevent further damage to the earth?

2. What does it mean to be good stewards of the Earth?
Share some of the plans that you are engaged with to begin
cleaning up our earth.

3. What part will you take in reducing our garbage? As a
consumer, what will you do to reduce the overabundance of
packaging that so contributes to our Earth's garbage?

4. How will you honor and perpetuate the goodness of
God's creation?

Chapter Thirteen

Building Relationships

"Last Day"
Elisabeth Sophia Lee

"No one has greater love than this, to lay down one's life for one's friends."

- JOHN 15:13

I love visiting family in Canada during the summer. The last day of our visit, I am always very sad. A few summers ago, on my last day in Canada, I woke up with a sorrowful feeling all over my body. I didn't want to leave. I woke up really early, before my cousin Naomi got up. I made my bed neatly and went to the kitchen. Though we had plenty of time before we left, I couldn't fall back asleep, so I decided to wait in the library on the main floor thinking that Naomi would go there first when she got up and we could spend our last few minutes together. But she didn't wake up.

To kill time, I made sure I had packed all of my belongings. Then I checked all the rooms in the house, making sure nobody's things were left behind. Then, my brothers woke up and double-checked their things. I could hear my dad coming in and out of the house, packing the car for our eight-hour drive back home to Pennsylvania. I went on Naomi's laptop to check whether I had any emails from my mom who was traveling herself. There were none.

Soon, it was time to leave. I carried my things to our van and packed them next to my seat. Naomi still was not up, and I was a little disappointed. I couldn't give her a proper goodbye, but I was sure we would see each other soon. We said goodbye to my aunt, uncle, and my cousin Matthew, and my family and I got into the car for the long drive back to Pennsylvania.

As I reflect on our biannual trip to Toronto to visit family and friends, I realize that material things do not matter as much as relationships with people. I am always asking my mom for a phone, a new laptop, or new clothes to wear. I know these are not that important, yet I keep asking my mom for them! I know relationships are far more important and they are what keep us going. As I go through troubling times at school or with dance, I know I have family and friends who will support me and always comfort me and keep me going. I am grateful to God for what I have. I have to stop asking for things that are not that important and can damage the earth.

"Walls that Divide"
Grace Ji-Sun Kim

"And he brought me to the entrance of the court; I looked, and there was a hole in the wall."

- Ezekiel 8:7

A few years ago, I took a seminary class to the Mexico-U.S. border through Borderlinks, an organization that provides educational experiences to connect divided communities, raise awareness about border and immigration policies and their impact, and inspire people to act for social transformation. We visited the metal wall that separates the United States from Mexico at Nogales, Mexico.

These walls went up in 1994.

The North American Free Trade Agreement (NAFTA), established in 1994, was intended to foster trade and the economic status of Mexico. However, it failed to do this. It backfired and made the economic situation worse for the people of Mexico. The foreign-owned factories polluted Mexico, and Mexican farmers lost their livelihoods as it became too difficult to fight against the American farmers. Rich corporations and companies benefited the most from the Free Trade Agreement thanks to being able to move their factories down to Mexico where the labor was cheap and profits higher. As the economy of Mexico suffered, and people were unable to make a living with affordable wages from the factories, more people made their way, without documents, to the United States seeking work to support their families.

In 2006, the United States responded with the

Secure Fence Act. As President George W. Bush signed the bill, he stated, "This bill will help protect the American people. This bill will make our borders more secure. It is an important step toward immigration reform." The act included provisions for the construction of physical barriers — walls — and the use of technology to these ends. This is uncomfortably similar to the famous Berlin Wall, constructed between East and West Berlin, by the Soviets, in 1961, and gleefully torn down in 1989, when the city was reunited.

This wall is under constant surveillance to prevent people from entering the U.S. illegally. Ironically, it is a wall built from scraps of metal landing strips from the Gulf War. The border is militarized with patrols who treat migrants as "prisoners of war." It symbolizes greed, xenophobia, pride, nonsense, and fear of the other, a reminder of wanting to protect what is yours and not sharing what God has given you. Walls continue to go up along the border as the people of the United States continue to fear that undocumented people will take away jobs. Even presidential candidates talk about building walls – very tall walls, across the entire U.S. and Mexican border to prevent anyone from illegally entering the U.S.. President Trump wants to build an even bigger wall and wants Mexico to pay for it. Such xenophobic actions may devastate the lives of the poor in both countries because in many ways, it is the U.S. that has made Mexico and Central American countries poor.

As we ponder walls and the devastation caused by building them by creating climate change havoc, flooding, animals unable to migrate in search of food, and making it nearly impossible for migrant workers to find work in the U.S., many people in the United States have begun to recognize that we cannot continue building walls to separate us from others. Rather, we need to break them down.

The Korean peninsula is another example of a place that is divided by a great wall/barrier. The divided border is called the DMZ: a "demilitarized zone," created in 1953, years after Korea was separated into two countries by the United States and the Soviet Union at the end of World War II. This division continues to generate great fear and hostility.

I have visited the DMZ several times. The last time, I took two of my three children to see it. They are too young to remember the visit, but every time I visit the DMZ, I am overcome with emotion. I am overwhelmed at the thought of the devastation the DMZ has caused--of families separated, lives lost, friendships broken, and a country torn apart. It symbolizes despair, hatred, sadness, anger, division, and hopelessness.

At the border, there is a metal fence that divides the road traveling into the DMZ. Hundreds of letters, notes, flowers, and trinkets are woven into the fence, left by families and strangers to express the pain and longing that each person feels. Koreans want the two Koreas to unite so that the wall can be dismantled and families reunited. There is a deep longing among them for healing of their national brokenness.

For such walls of division to come down we need to repair the damaged relationships that built them in the first place. Re-establishing communication, trust, and mutuality is hard work, whether it is in my homeland of the Korean peninsula or between the U.S. and Mexico. Long years of division have only made both the distrust and the longing more entrenched. But the dismantling of the Berlin wall reminds us it is possible.

There are also walls that we build around ourselves and each other. Walls that destroy people and communities. We build them out of fear of each other. We are afraid of those who have different cultures or faith traditions or sexuality. Due to such baseless fears, we build up walls to separate us from 'them'. But these walls only build further inequity, distrust and devastation. We must learn to trust God and break down the walls of separation and learn to embrace one another.

Reflections:

1. What are some of the walls that you have built up in your own life? What originally prompted you to build those walls? What caused the fear, anger, or hardship that began the process of cementing those divisions in your life?

2. How can we start dismantling the walls and the emotions that have fortified them and instead build trust, harmony, and love?

3. What ingredients will help us establish a more just society and build each other up rather than tear each other down?

Chapter Fourteen

Future

"My Dream of a Better Future"
Elisabeth Sophia Lee

"David danced before the Lord with all his might; David was girded with a linen ephod. So David and all the house of Israel brought up the ark of the Lord with shouting, and with the sound of the trumpet."

- 2 SAMUEL 6:14-15

God gives us a talent, a talent to use for God. I believe that everyone has a talent and is passionate about something. People have goals and dreams about who they want to be in the future. Sometimes due to lack of money, opportunity, or encouragement people cannot achieve their goals or dreams.

My mother tells my brothers and me how lucky we are growing up with lots of opportunities and with parents "like them." My dad is a mathematics professor, so he can always help us in math, chemistry, and physics. My mother is a theology professor and can help with the social sciences and with editing our homework and assignments.

My mother never fails to remind us of the many reasons we are lucky. She never received much support from her parents, who were immigrants, and didn't have the connections or social and cultural advantages to help her and her sister. Her parents didn't speak English well and never knew what was happening outside the home. They were unable to provide my mother and her sister the opportunities I have as they had neither money nor resources.

I used to cringe every time my mother told us about her childhood and its missed opportunities and hardships. Now that I am a teenager, I am coming to understand her situation better and appreciate my own opportunities as I consider my dream.

For me, that dream is to be a dancer. Dancing is my life, my dream, and my future. I've been dancing since the age of three and, since then, my passion and love for it has grown. It started at the YMCA in Bethlehem, Pennsylvania, when my mother signed me up for the community dance class. I loved dancing in the class. After a year of dance classes at the YMCA, I moved to a ballet school called "Kathleen A. Magyar" to work with more serious dancers and teachers. After a few years, I changed schools to the Ballet Guild of the Lehigh Valley, which has classes in pre-professional ballet for serious dancers. There I dance ballet, pointe, and jazz. For the past six years, I have been dancing six classes a week for two to five hours a day.

Since I was seven I've danced in The Nutcracker with The Ballet Guild of the Lehigh Valley. The auditions start in September, and rehearsals run from October until the performances in December. Overall, these all add up to a lot of rehearsals and sometimes I dance the same role two or three years in a row. Understandably people ask me, "Doesn't going to rehearsals get boring – doing the same thing over and over?" "No, it doesn't," I reply.

And yet, as a dancer, almost always my blistered feet hurt, my back aches, and I have to make sure I'm eating the right food. Besides the physical pain, there's also the enormous time commitment. Indeed, why do I continue to dance?

Something deep within my heart gets a strong sense of satisfaction from dancing and performing. I feel content and experience great joy from dancing. Being on stage energizes and enlivens me. I enjoy the experience of dancing while hundreds of people watch my every move. The lights and attention on me during my time on stage make me feel great—not only does it bring me pleasure, but I bring pleasure to the audience.

I love looking glamorous and beautiful in costumes with my hair and make-up done. I love the experience of performing my best and entertaining the audience. It fills my heart with deep joy and a sense of accomplishment. The whole production is memorable. Not just my particular part in it. I never tire of the whole experience of dancing.

This brings me to my next dream, which is to help others and give back to my community. Hopefully, I can do both through my dancing.

As I think about my mother's childhood, I realize not everyone is as lucky as I am. My mother's struggles help me understand the multiple layers of hardships involved in trying to adjust to this country and trying to make it here. I hope to offer free dance classes for younger children who cannot afford to take classes. I hope to raise money through dancing and teaching dance to help those who do not have food to eat or a place to live. I want to use my dancing talent to do something to make our world a little better in whatever way I can.

Giving or changing little things one day at a time can make a difference in our world. Little things can put big smiles on dozens of faces. To do that through my dancing is my dream.

"Our Children's Future"
Grace Ji-Sun Kim

"Train children in the right way, and when old, they will not stray."

- PROVERBS 22:6

Being a parent is hard work. I never imagined it to be as hard as it is. Before I had any children, I thought "feed them well" and they will grow up to be good people. I did not imagine I would have to discipline them 24/7, fret over their fighting amongst themselves, stress out about them not doing their homework, or argue with them constantly about everything under the sun.

I imagined parenting to be easy because my sister and I grew up with "hands-off parents" who didn't have much input into our lives, due to their inability to speak English well and lack of resources and cultural understanding.

I have become the opposite of my parents. I am very much a hands-on parent. I want to raise children who will do something meaningful with their lives that makes a deep impact on society. I feel a lot of pressure to get my own work of teaching and research done, and of making sure that my three children are doing well.

One of the things I always wanted to do as a child was take ballet lessons. The only lessons I received were piano lessons. The excitement of taking piano lessons wore off after about three months. At the beginning, I couldn't wait to take them. I begged my parents to sign us up for lessons. I begged them to buy a piano. Since we were so poor, we couldn't buy a piano right away, so I practiced on our parquet floor, pretending the strips of parquet were piano keys and making my own piano sounds as I moved my fingers over the floor. My dad finally bought a used, brown, upright piano. It was old and out of tune all the time. Even though we got it professionally tuned, there was always a faint humming sound in the background each time we played.

Piano proved difficult and exhausting for me. Then I began to yearn to learn ballet. My family attended a big old Presbyterian church in downtown Toronto that had huge organ pipes at the front of the sanctuary. It also had an education wing, one room of which had been converted into a ballet studio. When I went for mid-week youth meetings, I would see the ballet students getting changed and going into their classes. I saw the ballet slippers and the outfits and I wished my parents had the money for ballet lessons when I was a child. Unfortunately, it never happened. I never got a chance.

So when my daughter was born, I immediately thought, once she is old enough to walk, I will enroll her in ballet classes. When she was three, the youngest age they would take students, I signed her up in ballet class at the YMCA. She loved it.

Not only did she love it but she was a good dancer! She followed directions and was able to carry out the intricate moves correctly. When many of her dance friends started dropping out, she stayed on. She is still dancing now, over twelve years later. Her ballet instructors keep pushing her (and trying to convince me) to go into ballet professionally, as she has nice long legs and is a great dancer. I always tell them that this is only a hobby and she will not do it professionally. It is too difficult a life. Instead, I encourage her to pursue a career in the scientific or mathematical fields.

Many Asian American moms want their children to study sciences so that they will get into some sort of medical profession. It is a more stable job in society. Even if there is an economic downturn, everybody needs a doctor and thus doctors can always find employment.

As a parent, I struggle between what my children want to do versus what I think they should be doing. I think this is a dilemma for many parents and their children. Part of this struggle is about communication and understanding one another, a struggle typically not helped by technological gadgets that have replaced more personal ways of having face to face contact with one another.

Parenting is not easy. It's not one thing you master. It is a constantly changing, evolving skill, as kids get older and have new needs. No magic wand takes away the pain and struggle that parents and children experience as they try their best to stay in touch with each other. But we must not give up.

Reflections:

1. Share some of your personal dreams or goals.

2. Do you quarrel with your parents about what you want to do with your life? Are your parents' expectations different from your own dreams? How do you cope with that?

3. How can we praise God through what we choose to do with our lives, professionally or otherwise?

4. What are some of the joys of parenting? And what are some of the difficulties? How can we mitigate these painful realities of parenting?

5. What ideas do you have to allow children to follow their own dreams and not our dreams for them?

6. Sharing with our child(ren) what is difficult about parenting them can sometimes work well. Can you recall a time when it paid dividends for you and your relationships with your child(ren)?

7. What can we do to make the future brighter for the next generation?

Chapter Fifteen

Social Media

"On My Phone"
Elisabeth Sophia Lee

"Two are better than one, because they have a good reward for their toil. For if they fall, one will lift up the other; but woe to one who is alone and falls and does not have another to help."

- ECCLESIASTES 4:9-10

My mother and I struggle constantly about what is an appropriate use of social media. She complains about my Internet and social media usage. We are forever bickering about me getting off my phone and my wanting to stay on it a bit more. She considers it a waste of time and tells me to read a book instead. Whenever she says this, I roll my eyes and ignore her. But in my better moments I know that I have to be selective about how I use social media. I try.

Things like Instagram® and Snapchat® teach me things. People say that a picture is worth a thousand words and I like to think that it is. Instagram has many pages that post pictures of interesting things. Without it, I would not have known that New York City will turn their old phone booths into Wi-Fi hot spots or that 85 percent of the Chinese population share only 100 surnames, and that of these "Li" and "Zhang" covers 13 percent of the Chinese population.

Snapchat® includes a "Discover page" that takes you to different pages like ESPN, People, CNN, and National

Geographic. Every day, each page is updated with the newest articles or information about the world. And every day, I go to "Discover" and read the "CNN" reports. This is where I learn most of current things that are occurring all around the world. It is convenient to be able to communicate with friends and learn new things all through one app!

Social media is how most of the people I know share news, connect with old friends, and make new online friends. It will probably be part of our school curriculum. Whatever it may be or become, I hope that I can use it somehow to do God's work. Social media can be a medium to share the good news with God's people. It can be a way to fight for equality and fight for justice. I know some adults are already using it for such means. People are using hashtags to raise awareness and to fight against racism and sexism that arises in our society. My mother fills me in sometimes of the new hashtags that come up to fix social injustices. Senator Elizabeth Warren who spoke up against the nomination of Jeff Sessions as Attorney General by reading a letter from the late Coretta Scott King, was silenced. A new hashtag emerged "#letlizspeak" to allow Warren to speak up against Sessions.

I believe it is a good way to join in and publicize social and Christian activism. I need to be more engaged and be more active in this realm. My mom always told me that the "personal is political" and therefore we need to get involved in social justice issues. I know social media has to go beyond just connecting with friends and to really being with each other and being with one another.

I am constantly thinking about how social media can be helpful. I am hoping that my mother will stop telling me to get off my phone and that she will realize I am learning something which will enable me to make our world a better place!

The Church in a Media-Saturated Society[1]
Grace Ji-Sun Kim

"Now you are the body of Christ and individually members of it."

- 1 CORINTHIANS 12:27

I grew up in the days of the encyclopedia salesman. I clearly remember the day when a clean-cut, well-dressed man knocked on our apartment door to sell us the twenty-six-volume World Book Encyclopedia. We were recent immigrants and could not speak English fluently. We had few worldly possessions and the last thing we needed in our house was a twenty-six-volume encyclopedia.

After the one-hour presentation during which we flipped through the volumes full of exciting information, my dad said no. The salesman looked sad and pitiful as he packed up his sales kit and realized that he wasted over an hour to try to convince us to buy the set. As he exited the door, he gave one last pitch and, suddenly, my dad changed his mind and we bought the whole set.

Either the salesman was good or my parents had this strong desire that their children needed to know "everything there is to know about the world." Maybe it was a bit of both.

Today, long gone are those enormous encyclopedias that once filled the bookshelves of many of my childhood friends' homes. Now we have everything we need to know at our fingertips through iPads, computers, cell phones, or

[1] A small portion of this piece first appeared in my chapter, "Writing Publicly" in *Writing Theologically*, edited by Eric Barreto (Minneapolis: Fortress Press, 2015), 73-86.

other gadgets. We live in a media-saturated society. We no longer need twenty-six bulky volumes to help us understand the world. Now, all we need is a palm-sized gadget to find the latest news, the juiciest gossip, or the up-to-date facts on anything under the sun.

Now information surrounds us all day long. Things we may not want to read or watch seem to appear on our computer screens or on billboards as we drive along the highways. What does it mean for us, and especially for our children to live in a media-saturated society with all this information?

First, we should be concerned about the easy accessibility of media and how messages are disseminated and how it affects our children. One might observe that the accuracy of what we see has decreased in proportion to the volume of information we have available. This is especially true of memes seen on Facebook and other forms of social media. It is also a risk with seemingly objective sources such as Wikipedia, on which we rely so frequently to look up old and new ideas alike. Encyclopedia articles were carefully edited for accuracy and they were written with cool heads with no need to accentuate the spectacular. Neither of those factors is at work in much of the information foisted upon us. We want our children to be able to discern what is good and what is acceptable to them and to be able to weed out unnecessary, unhealthy, and inaccurate information.

Second, it is important not to get overwhelmed by the media-saturated society and to exercise self-discipline. We can waste hours on the Internet chatting with Facebook friends, checking Twitter, or just surfing the net. The time can evaporate like the water in an unattended teapot on a flame. Social media exerts a constant tug, as we want to work, to remain close, both physically and emotionally, with friends, colleagues, and family.

Third, the challenge is to use social media to our advantage, such as to build the church and our theological seminaries. How can we swim in it, without drowning? How can we can make media work for us? As a theologian and ordained minister, I know it is important we try to make use of media to help share news of hope, justice, peace, and love. Chances are, there are more people in the media-saturated world listening to us than people sitting in our pews and classrooms.

Social media gives us an additional podium and pulpit. The media has become the backdrop and the medium of our messages. More people read media reports than read our theological textbooks. More listen to and view media outlets than hear our sermons. That means that our message from the pulpit may be out of touch with those secular sources. If so, our message will not be taken seriously.

The sooner the church and seminaries catch on to this, the better equipped we will become to serve the church and the world today. With the decline in seminary enrollment and church membership, the use of media may now become more than just an attraction to draw in younger members; it may soon become a matter of survival for our churches and seminaries. It brings people together to join in the kin-dom participation—meaning to build a more inclusive and loving community of God. The key is for churches and seminaries to become known as a reliable media source where information content is high, accurate, and easy to reach. It should also be a source for enlightenment, meditation, and reflection – up to date, and free of charge to those who have the most rudimentary tablet, phone, or iPod. If we attract their interest and make it easy to access, people will pay attention to our message.

Reflections:

1. How does social media impact you--in negative and positive ways?

2. In what ways is social media an effective means of communication?

3. How do you use social media in your day-to-day life?

4. Have you considered using social media for God's work? What might that look like?

5. What are some of the pitfalls of using social media for worship, Bible study, small group meetings? What are the advantages and the disadvantages of social media?

Conclusion: Church and our Christian Faith

We live in a postcolonial world where people are migrating for all kinds of reasons, creating climate, political, religious, and economic refugees. In our world of unrelenting movement, we inevitably encounter more and more people of different cultures, languages and faiths. As we do, it is important to embrace one another, especially with those who are seemingly so different from us.

Climate change is an incredibly consequential element of both the human race and the context of our world as a whole. Unless we learn to live sustainably, we will soon squander the very resources that have supported life on earth. I imagine that within twenty years, economics, religion, sexism, and racism will all be seen in terms of climate change and sustainability.

Social media has somehow become a necessary evil. We can't seem to live without it, but it can become a hazard if we don't manage it well. Social media can take valuable time away from ourselves and our families as we get sucked into all the available information on our fingertips about many nonessential and unimportant facts. But if we can harness it properly, we can use it for social justice and for building the kin-dom of God. How we go about using social media is a choice we make daily.

Understanding our past and our present helps us to plan for the future. Once we come to terms with our reality, perhaps we will have the impetus to forgo some of our destructive habits and work together for a more hopeful and sustainable future.

Concluding Thoughts
Grace Ji-Sun Kim & Elisabeth Sophia Lee

Mother-daughter conversations between us are some of our most cherished moments. Even through tumultuous times, they sustain us and keep us connected. Some families lose these intimate relationships due to strain, differences, and failure to find common ground. However, when these relationships are nurtured, they can bloom into some of the most beautiful and valuable relationships.

Our personal reflections in this book on marriage, death, discrimination, trust, faith, social media and climate change are attempts to open the dialogue between family members and communities. We shared some of our vulnerabilities and our pains in hopes that this kind of sharing will encourage you to engage in similar intimate dialogue with others.

This book arose from our desire to have a more open conversation with one another as mother and daughter. The journey of writing this book has been fun, hard work, frustrating, and broadening. It challenged some of our assumptions of the other and the world and made us reflect critically on one another's experiences. The collaboration has brought us both joy, laughter, and love and we hope it will spur conversations of your own.

"Three Personas"
by Theodore Andrew Lee

As the end of August approaches the stress builds up
The remembrance of late nights sitting in front of a messy
desk, taking large dosages of caffeine to help me through
the night.
Waking up at 4:30 in the morning to study,
as if I was a machine,
struggling to stay awake during school
with only the reward of good grades and the approval of my
parents. Tests, piles of homework, projects, and extra-curric-
ulars
fill my afternoons, forcing me to
manage my time and become focused.
The high expectations of my teachers and peers
make me even more studious.
I am a zombie,
immobilized from doing anything else.
School takes over and becomes
one of my three personas.
As I sit there, in that hard wooden chair,
the light emitting from my lamp beaming on my face,
I wish, only wish I could escape this hell.
A new mindset takes over as my eyes slowly drift togeth-
er...
I am free
The weather outside is fair, with only patches of clouds
I have no worries.
I am free
from the chains that bound me in my room for hours.
But,
there is a need for acceptance and approval
from those all around me.
There is a drive within me to be popular.

Going out late at night, to hang out with friends
staying out until whenever seemed right,
making rude jokes;
disregarding any rules.
My apathy rises exponentially.
I am blind to the people I am hurting.
This desire for an exciting social life
changes my personality and also becomes
one of my three personas.
I scream and escape this nightmare.
There must be something good in life.
Why must everything good, end up bad?
I pause and think…
I look around the room
and just outside the realm of light my lamp produces,
I spot my Bible.
The many retreats and services flash through my mind.
Dimmed lights, repentance and love in the air;
heartwarming praise touched my heart.
The many pains I have gone through brings doubt.
Has God always really been there?
Is he doing this for a purpose?
He has changed me.
He makes me look up to Him.
God produces
one of my three personas.
As I lie in bed and contemplate,
I begin to think about who I really am.
I am affected by my environment and my emotional state.
And I have three personas.
But regardless,
I am these hardships,
I am these desires,
I am my doubts.
This is me.